Accessible
Mathematics

Accessible Mathematics

10 Instructional Shifts
That Raise Student Achievement

Steven Leinwand

HEINEMANN
Portsmouth, NH

Heinemann
361 Hanover Street
Portsmouth, NH 03801–3912
www.heinemann.com

Offices and agents throughout the world

The author and publisher wish to thank those who have generously given permission to reprint borrowed material:

Appendix 3, "Research Matters / Teach Mathematics Right the First Time" by Steve Leinwand and Steve Fleischman was originally published in *Educational Leadership* (Volume 62, Number 1, September 2004). Reprinted by permission of the Association for Supervision and Curriculum Development.

Credits continue on page 113.

Library of Congress Cataloging-in-Publication Data

Leinwand, Steven.
    Accessible mathematics : ten instructional shifts that raise student achievement / Steven Leinwand.
        p. cm.
    Includes bibliographical references.
    ISBN-13: 978-0-325-02656-5
    ISBN-10: 0-325-02656-4
    1. Mathematics—Study and teaching.   2. Effective teaching.   I. Title.
QA11.2.L45 2009
510.71—dc22   2008047626

Editor: Emily Michie Birch
Production service: Matrix Productions Inc.
Production coordinator: Lynne Costa
Cover design: Joni Doherty
Typesetter: Aptara
Manufacturing: Valerie Cooper

Printed in the United States of America on acid-free paper
16   15   VP   9   10

*To the thousands of teachers of mathematics
who have welcomed me into their classrooms,
and
with love, to Ann, the best teacher I know.*

Contents

Introduction

It's Instruction That Matters Most

Fortunately, we all agree that our goal should be to ensure that all students know, like, and are able to apply mathematics as a direct result of their school experiences. Unfortunately, we also agree that as a country, we are currently falling far short of this goal. It's a tough situation for which many solutions have been suggested. However, of all the programs, initiatives, and proposals for addressing this situation, I'm increasingly convinced that the answer is one word: *instruction*. That is, the web of plans, actions, and decisions that constitute what teachers actually do behind closed classroom doors makes all the difference.

There is no question that a coherent and rational curriculum guides and organizes an effective mathematics program. Life is a lot easier when the assessments we use, or are subjected to, are closely aligned with this curriculum and hold us accountable for important mathematics. It certainly helps to have sufficient access to print and non-print materials that support implementation of the program. And it's a relief when we have supportive and gutsy leadership and parental support. But none of these program components has anything like the degree of impact on student achievement as the *quality of instruction*. For many reasons, no component of the K–12 mathematics program seems to get as little attention as instruction—the day in and day out of complex interactions between teachers and students that determine who learns how much mathematics.

As I noted in the conclusion of *Sensible Mathematics: A Guide for School Leaders,*

> Never stray from a *dogged focus on classroom instruction.* Just as Bill Clinton won in 1992 in part by making "It's the economy, stupid!" a campaign mantra, for educators and educational policy makers at all levels, the appropriate mantra must be "It's the classroom, stupid!" When all is said and done, it's not the buses, nor the buildings, nor the budgets that determine how much and how well students learn, it's the daily interaction between teachers and students, and among students,

in the classrooms of every school that determine how much and how well students will learn. . . . If one seeks to improve the quality of education and the quality of student achievement, enhancing, empowering, energizing, and engaging teaching and teachers has always been and will continue to be the method of choice.

This book begins where *Sensible Mathematics* ended. It focuses on mathematics instruction and is designed to give practical meaning to the challenges of "enhancing, empowering, energizing, and engaging" our teaching of mathematics.

I've been blessed by the opportunities that have been presented to me. For the past 30 years, as consultant, as evaluator, and as researcher, I've observed over 2000 mathematics classes from kindergarten to calculus. I've marveled at a fourth-grade teacher who artfully used the explanations of her students to summarize (and assess) the key understanding that emerged from a rotation through four fraction activity stations. I've been in awe of middle school teachers whose planning and classroom management routines kept students thoroughly engaged in mathematical thinking for 47 uninterrupted minutes. And I've been wowed by the diversity of approaches to solving a problem that is cultivated in classes that tangibly value multiple ways of thinking.

But I've also seen hundreds of missed opportunities and less than stellar lessons. I once watched a teacher direct the students to copy 15 word problems out of their textbook—a task that consumed all 42 minutes of class time. I've seen lessons where it was patently obvious that the teacher had not worked out the well-chosen problems the night before and had no idea what opportunities and stumbling blocks lay in the path to getting the right answer. And I've observed many lessons where so much time was essentially wasted going over the correct answers to homework problems that not enough time remained to address the day's new content effectively.

In other words, I've been given a rich repository of "data" from which to extract and synthesize what appears to work and what appears to make a difference. We've all heard that "the most important variable in determining the quality of education is the teacher." Of course that's true. But the next (and far more important) message is that it is instruction—what teachers actually do to present mathematical ideas and to structure learning—that makes all the difference.

The perspective I take is that increasing calls for greater accountability and the pressures of *No Child Left Behind*, to say nothing of our own personal professional expectations, require us to do something that, as a society, we've never before accomplished: taking this body of knowledge and skills called mathematics and presenting it in ways that result in all or nearly all students being successful. We know that this goal cannot be met by continuing to do what we have always done. We know that traditional and typical approaches rarely work for more than half of our students. We know we can't sprinkle in the same mathematics more gently and with bigger smiles, or pound it in harder and say it louder, and expect things to be different. We know that moving faster and mandating more and more mathematics earlier and earlier only exacerbate the problem for many. But most of all, we know that the only way we'll achieve our goal of broader and deeper mathematical literacy is by changing some of what we expect students to learn and a lot of how we go about teaching it. In other words, the goal of more math for more students is inextricably linked to teaching the math in distinctly different ways from how we were taught.

The good news is that we've got clear answers for how to do this. There are ways of shifting instructional practice that enhance our productivity and our effectiveness. This book focuses on exactly those shifts and strategies that make a difference and guides the provision of exactly the high-quality mathematics instruction that can and does work for far more students.

We've Got Most of the Answers

Walk into a kindergarten or first-grade classroom. You're likely to see kids actively engaged, often in play, learning by doing, and sponging up knowledge. They learn about shapes by seeing them all around their classroom. They name and refer to these shapes naturally and in context—not just in Chapter 7. They use materials to join and separate sets in ways that concretize numbers and operations. It's no surprise that, mathematically speaking, kindergarten and first-grade students tend to be a whole lot more successful than students in any other grades.

Look at typical reading instruction. In a large proportion of reading lessons, literal comprehension is nearly always extended to inferential and evaluative comprehension via a systematic progression of questions. As we'll explore in Chapter 3, it's not a surprise that for many students, reading is a far more positive, and more successful, experience than mathematics. Then wander into the gifted classroom and observe the questioning, the focus on reasoning, the frequent use of "Why?" and the attention paid to alternative approaches. It doesn't take much imagination to recognize the chasm between standard operating procedure in most gifted classes and the worksheet-driven, procedure-oriented drudgery that typically passes for mathematics instruction in the remedial class down the hall. In fact, stroll down the corridor of nearly any school, and you have an immediate sense of which classrooms you would hope your own children would be in. These are the active classes, the questioning classes, the thinking and reasoning classes where students are mentally, and even physically, engaged in the tasks at hand. You can feel the minds-on behaviors and sense the learning going on. And when we look deeper at what explains this engagement and this enhanced learning, whether in first grade or in a reading lesson or a gifted class, we can identify a clear pattern of instructional practices and behaviors that account for this success.

In other words, we know that there are places throughout the educational system where things tend to work consistently better than they do for mathematics. If this is the case, it becomes our job to identify and extract the specific strategies that are used in these successful places and experiences and to ensure that they are employed broadly and regularly to raise achievement, to improve instruction, and to make a difference in mathematics instruction for kids.

None of this is news. When instruction is traditional, rule-oriented teaching by telling and is devoid of number sense, we shouldn't be surprised when students announce that the 5% tax on a $12 shirt is $60. Alan Schoenfeld describes relating to students that a shepherd was guarding his flock of 18 sheep when all of a sudden 4 wolves came over the mountain. He then asks them, "How old is the shepherd?" This tends to evoke such appropriate answers as "Who knows?" and "That's silly!" from the majority of first graders and the depressing answer "22" from the majority of sixth graders. We do not need any more compelling evidence that something is seriously amiss. It is clear that for many students, thinking, reasoning, and sense-making are systematically exorcized from teaching because the primary focus in too many classrooms is a mindless emphasis on the one right way to get the one right answer to yet another decontextualized exercise.

Indeed, there are several ways to teach mathematics. We can demonstrate, tell, and let our students practice, or we can engage and focus on understanding and application. Nowhere is the traditional approach more succinctly presented than in *Everybody Counts,* the 1989 epic "Report to the Nation on the Future of Mathematics Education" from the National Research Council, where we are reminded that evidence from many sources shows that the least effective mode for mathematics learning is the one that prevails in most of America's classrooms: lecturing and listening. Despite daily homework, for most students and most teachers mathematics continues to be primarily a passive activity: teachers prescribe; students transcribe. Students simply do not retain for long what they learn by imitation from lectures, worksheets, or routine homework. Presentation and repetition help students do well on standardized tests and lower-order skills, but they are generally ineffective as teaching strategies for long-term learning, for high-order thinking, and for versatile problem-solving. (57)

Nowhere are the differences in how we might teach mathematics clearer than in the findings of the TIMSS video study. In the original work, Jim Stigler and his colleagues videotaped one hundred randomly chosen eighth-grade classes in the United States, Germany, and Japan. The analysis of these videos revealed two very different cultural scripts for what typically takes place in a mathematics classroom. Not surprisingly, in the United States and Germany, the focus was on skill acquisition and the typical class proceeded as follows:

- The teacher instructs students in a concept or skill.
- The teacher solves example problems with the class.
- The students practice on their own while the teacher assists individual students.

Interestingly, in Japan, one finds a very different cultural script— not necessary a better script, but certainly different. In this case, the focus was on understanding and the typical class unfolded this way:

- The teacher poses a complex, thought-provoking problem.
- Students struggle with the problem.
- Various students present ideas or solutions to the class.
- The class discusses the various solution methods.
- The teacher summarizes the class' conclusions.
- The students practice similar problems.

If the traditional American mathematics classroom script is working for only about half of our students, one answer is to vary our approach. We are quick to acknowledge that our students come to us with incredibly diverse backgrounds, interests, and learning styles, but so often they are met with one monolithic approach best characterized as lecture and practice. It seems sensible that one way to address the diversity of our students is with greater diversity in our instructional practices. This diversity of practice implies variation in our approaches, alternative approaches to solving problems and thinking through the mathematics, and a richness of questioning that stimulates these alternatives and this thinking.

The sad reality is that our critics are not all wrong. For too long and for too many students the typical outcomes of school mathematics are mountains of math anxiety, tons of mathematical illiteracy, mediocre test scores, gobs of wasteful remediation, and a slew of entirely warranted criticism. This is not a pretty picture and is very hard to defensively dismiss. But the good news is that we know more than enough to avoid these outcomes. The better news is that we have sensible and accessible solutions. And the best news is that overcoming the obstacles to implementing these solutions does not require more money or expensive interventions, or numerous days of professional development, or more courses in mathematics content. The primary obstacle is a lack of direction and a lack of will to make a few powerful instructional shifts in how we plan, implement, and assess daily mathematics instruction. In short, the answers lie in narrowing the chasm between what we know and what we do!

What exactly are these shifts? I've identified ten that capture much of what I have observed and that appear to work.

1. Incorporate ongoing cumulative review into every day's lesson.

2. Adapt what we know works in our reading programs and apply it to mathematics instruction.

3. Use multiple representations of mathematical entities.

4. Create language-rich classroom routines.

5. Take every available opportunity to support the development of number sense.

6. Build from graphs, charts, and tables.

7. Tie the math to such questions as How big? How much? How far? to increase the natural use of measurement throughout the curriculum.

8. Minimize what is no longer important, and teach what is important when it is appropriate to do so.

9. Embed the mathematics in realistic problems and real-world contexts.

10. Make "Why?" "How do you know?" "Can you explain?" classroom mantras.

Shifts 1, 2, and 10 focus broadly on review, discourse, and stimulating a depth of understanding. Shifts 3, 4, and 5 address the use of representations, communication, and number sense—three critical domains for accessing and demonstrating mathematical understanding. Shifts 6, 7, and 9 ground the mathematics in the world in which we live and build understanding from data and measurement that apply key mathematical ideas. Finally, shift 8 reminds us that we can't do it all. Taken together, these ten strategies or shifts in how we plan, implement, and assess our mathematics instruction represent a road map for significantly enhancing the quality of our teaching and its impact on student achievement.

Ready, Set, Review

2

INSTRUCTIONAL SHIFT 1

Incorporate ongoing cumulative review into every day's lesson.

H ere is what every teacher knows: Almost no student masters something new after one or two lessons or one or two homework assignments. Skills, terms, and concepts are constantly being forgotten or confused. One student can't remember the product of 9 and 7. A class forgets that there are 16 ounces in a pint and in a pound. It is apparent that *isosceles* is a long-forgotten term when it elicits only a sea of blank stares.

These examples illustrate why one of the most effective strategies for fostering mastery and retention of critical mathematics skills and concepts is daily cumulative review. Some teachers call it opening exercises or denote it as daily launch strategies in their lesson plans. Others call it daily warm-ups or mini-math. Whatever the label, it's a daily, quick, systematically considered assessment that creates an immediate focus on mathematics. It's deliberate, ongoing, cumulative review. Some days it is just one or two word problems written on the board or flashed on a screen; other days it is seven quick oral questions; and other days it is five written questions to get things going. But over the course of a week it is a chance, depending on the grade, class, or course, to address a number fact of the day, an estimate of the day, a term of the day, a skill of the day, a picture of the day, and/or a measurement of the day.

Consider the start of a sixth-grade, second-period class. As soon as the kids are in the room, sometimes even before the bell rings, you welcome the class and announce, "Number from one to six." Already your class understands that you don't waste time dilly-dallying around with attendance or announcements or collecting homework when you've got only got 47 minutes a day for math. Your students now know that today's mini-math is a six-item oral quiz, and by the third week of school, based on the routines you've established, your students know that you'll read each question twice as you wander around the room taking attendance and/or checking that each student has completed last night's homework.

OCT. 14 MINI-MATH

Second Period

1. 6×7
2. What number is 1000 less than 18,294?
3. About how much is 29¢ and 32¢?
4. What is $\frac{1}{10}$ of 450?
5. Draw a picture of $1\frac{2}{3}$.
6. Estimate my weight in kilograms.

Let's listen in: "Good morning! Today's mini-math number is . . . (building anticipation) . . . SIX! Ready. One, two, three, four, five, six, let's go. Great. Come on, gang. Wonderful! Number one, what is six times seven? (Pause) Number one, for those of you who weren't listening, what is the product of six and seven? That's right, I read it a little differently the second time, but I promise you the answer didn't change. Ready? Number two, what number is 1000 less than 18,294? Oooh, you guys really got me worried last week when we needed to use our understanding of place value. I know we did that back in September, but this is too important to forget. Once again, number two, what number is 1000 less than 18,294? (Pause) Raise your hand if you need more time. Awesome. Number three, you went into a store and bought two items. One was 32 cents. The other was 29 cents and the question is, about how much did you spend? For those of you who don't yet love story problems, I'll make it very easy: Number three, about how much is 32 cents plus 29 cents? (Pause) Questions? I see none. That's great. Number four, what is one-tenth of 450? This is the question for which I need to see how well you do to help me decide where to start teaching today's class. Again, number four, what is zero point one times 450? (Pause) Remember, sometimes it helps to write down the question as well as the answer. Is everybody ready? Number five is today's pictorial daily double! Next to number five, would you please draw a picture that a normal human being could look at and say, 'Oh, my! Look at that! That's a picture of one and two-thirds.' Boys and girls, do you know what we call that in the teacher's room? We call that creating a pictorial representation of the mixed number known as one and two-thirds."

You wander around the room as one student shades in her circle. You notice another student whose rectangles are divided into three unequal pieces. You've also checked to see that last night's homework is completed and sitting on everyone's desk. Finally, since measurement is consistently the weakest topic on your school's state test results, and since you've become a complete compulsive measurement nut, you end with the question: "And finally, number six, about how much do I weigh *in kilograms*? Boys and girls, I'll give you a hint. I weigh about 185 pounds. Once again, what is my weight to the nearest kilogram? Go. (Pause) Remember, if you leave number six blank, you get a zero for the entire quiz. You are better off writing 10,000 than leaving number six blank. Put in an answer right now—four, three, two, one—done! Now please switch papers."

That's all there is to it. You've systematically covered six key understandings and you've got a slew of data, efficiently collected, that tells you the degree to which your students have these understandings. But the real teaching, in the form of review, formative assessment, and re-teaching, emerges when you do a quick review of the answers.

Number One: 6 × 7

You started with this question because you know that some of your students are still struggling with "harder" multiplication facts and their related division facts (6 × 7, 6 × 8, 6 × 9, 7 × 7, 7 × 8, 7 × 9, 8 × 8, 8 × 9, and 9 × 9). Since students have switched papers, a simple, "Raise your hand if the answer to number one is *not* 42" quickly and accurately tells you how many students are still struggling with 6 × 7. When it's down to just a few or even none, consider the positive reinforcement and foreshadowing of "Great progress. We're down to only two of you having problems with 6×7. By the way, the first question tomorrow will be 9×6. And the product is . . . ?"

Within the first few minutes of your class, you've

- taken affirmative action on fact mastery by testing one of the more troublesome multiplication facts
- ascertained the number of students who still don't have a command of this fact
- provided, if appropriate, positive reinforcement about the progress your class is making
- planted $9 \times 6 = 54$ into memory banks as preparation for tomorrow.

Number Two: What Number is 1000 Less Than 18,294?

You added this question to mini-math because it has been a month since you finished the place value chapter. You understand that a mature sense of place value emerges from more than questions like "What digit is in the tens place?" and "What is the value of the 8?" After quickly checking to see that most of your students have correctly answered 17,294, you can follow up with questions like "What digit did you change and why?" If many students miss this question, you can follow up with questions like "Okay, so what number is 100 more than 18,294?" If most students find this easy, you know you can challenge your students with questions requiring addition that involves changing the digit 9 to a 0 ("What number is 100 more than 2984?") or subtraction that involves changing the digit 0 to a 9 ("What number is 0.01 less than 9.102?)—questions that are much more difficult but capture a mature understanding of place value.

With questions like this, you have

- broadened place value to an understanding of 10, 100, 1000, and 10,000 more and less than a given number, and set the foundation for 0.1, 0.01, and 0.001 more and less than a number
- recognized that a topic taught one month earlier needs periodic attention and reinforcement
- supported the gradual development of number sense for all students.

Number Three: About How Much is 29 and 32?

Let's listen in again to how this might be handled. "Okay, number three. Help me with this. Look at the paper in front of you. Hopefully it's not your own paper. Raise your hand if the answer on the paper is 62. Wonderful. Full credit. Raise your hand if you have 61. Look at all the 61s in the class. That's great, also full credit. How many of you have 60? Does anyone have a paper with an answer other than 60, 61, or 62? Amazing. What do you have? 37? I don't think so, unless you can justify it. (Pause to await a justification that is unlikely to be compelling.) So we *do* have one wrong answer in the class. Okay, let me hear from you. How do you justify 62? (One student states that she rounded 29 to 30 and added 30 and 32 to get 62.) What about 61? (Another student states that it was easy enough to get the exact answer with mental math by adding 20 and 30 to get 50 and then 9 and 2 to get a total of 61) And 60? (A third student states that he rounded both numbers to 30 and added to get 60.) Nice work. Good justifications."

By incorporating at least one estimate every day, you have

- reinforced a commitment to estimation and the justification of all estimates
- clearly communicated that there are many correct approaches to arriving at an estimate
- supported a classroom culture that values the development of number sense that transcends a narrow focus on merely getting correct answers to exercises.

We know that we live in a world where estimation is the way in which smart kids show that they're smart. We know that they often use estimation to outsmart the test by eliminating ridiculous answers. We also know that the weaker kids are often taught—to their detriment—that there is a correct procedure to arrive at estimates, in the same way that there are correct computational procedures. We will return to this matter in Chapter 6.

Number Four: $\frac{1}{10}$ of 450

If one thinks about the calculations that we make in everyday life, at the store, the deli counter, the restaurant, and the gas station, we realize that after a command of basic addition, subtraction, multiplication, and division facts, the next most important and empowering mathematical skills are multiplying and dividing numbers by 10, 100 and 1000. Asking students to find $\frac{1}{10}$ of 450 or 52 times 100 or 8.35 ÷ 10 reinforces (and, if necessary, re-teaches) the critical understanding of moving decimal points to the left to get smaller and to the right to get bigger, as well as the relationship between one, two, and three places and $\frac{10}{0.1}$, $\frac{100}{0.01}$, and $\frac{1000}{0.001}$, respectively.

When students correctly respond "45," the follow-up is a simple three-question barrage:

- Are you getting bigger or smaller? Why? ("Smaller because $\frac{1}{10}$ of a number reduces its magnitude.")
- So does the decimal move to the left or the right? Why? ("To the left because you're getting smaller.")
- And how many places must you move the decimal point? Why? ("Only one place because it's 10.")

Consider the cumulative power of a quick multiply or divide by 10, 100, 1000 or by 0.1, 0.01 or 0.001 every other week, in addition to when it arises as part of the problems and explanations that are part of your core instruction. Consider the development of understanding that dividing by 10 is the same as multiplying by 0.1 or that multiplying by 100 is the same as dividing by 0.01. And consider how this practical approach to formative assessment gives students a clear sense of their own progress as they recognize that skills and understandings that were weak or missing at one point can become clear and "second nature" over time.

Number Five: Draw a Picture of $1\frac{2}{3}$

As we will see in Chapter 4, one of the most powerful tools we have to help students develop conceptual understanding of key mathematical ideas is concretizing the mathematics by means of pictures and visualization. Just as the use of representations is a critical component of all good instruction, mini-math is the perfect opportunity to reinforce this idea. It's amazingly informative to see what proportion of your class turns to circles or pizza pies or rectangles and how many use a measurement model like rulers or measuring cups. It's humbling to see how many create equal-sized thirds and how many still fail to understand this critical piece of the fraction puzzle.

If there is time, or if there is clear misunderstanding, I often follow up with "Okay. Please describe the picture on the paper in front of you." When one student says, "There are two circles," I often draw on the board two non-congruent circles to raise the issue that the wholes must be equal in size. When another student says, "Divide the circle into three parts," I often divide the circle in half and then divide one of the halves in half to lighten things up as well as raise the issue of equal parts. It's also amazing how much geometry can be reviewed (and even taught) when students must describe the pictures that one of their classmates has created to show a fraction or a decimal or a geometric figure. For example, "Draw a circle, now draw a radius, then go 120° and draw another radius…."

Number Six: My Weight in Kilograms

Finally, as we will see in Chapter 8, measurement is often the lost strand of the mathematics curriculum. And if measurement is lost, metric measurement is missing in action altogether. Consider the blood that needs to flow to the brain early in each class to estimate the weight of the math textbook in pounds or the length of the bulletin board in centimeters or the area of the school cafeteria in square feet. Consider the sinking feeling of helplessness when a student is confronted with estimating my weight in kilograms. One hopes that by now, some of the students have developed the referent that their weight is about 50 kilograms, so I must weigh about 100 kilograms. Or one would hope that students have developed a gut sense that, just as a liter is about a quart, a kilogram is about 2 pounds, so if I weight 185 pounds, I must weigh about 90 kilograms. Because we're looking for understanding and for ballpark estimates of these measures, I often provide a reasonable range and announce that any answer between 50 and 120 gets full credit. Gradually, over the course of the year, and depending on what is being measured and what units are being asked for, you can reduce the range of acceptable answers.

I then expect students to grade the paper they've been given from 0 to 6 and hand it back to the student whose paper it is for a quick look-see, and then I collect the batch for my own quick look-see.

By now it should be clear that I'm compulsive about estimation. I'm obsessive about asking students "why" and about measurement. And I'm committed to helping students visualize mathematics. Daily review is one of many ways to act on my compulsions and broaden the scope of any single lesson beyond a narrow focus on the day's major objective.

Another way to view the 5 to 8 minutes allocated to this daily activity is to consider that 5 minutes × 180 days equals 900 minutes, or 15 hours! You know that you can change the world in 15 hours. Consider that 15 hours is about half a college course. Or think about how much can be accomplished in 15 one-hour tutoring sessions. It boggles the minds of many teachers and tutors that you can often cover much of an Algebra I course in 10 one-hour sessions and do it well. So in fact, these 5 minutes a day are roughly equivalent to half an hour per week of tutoring for an entire semester.

It should be clear that the specific content of mini-math is easily modified to accommodate the expectations for second graders and for algebra students.

Late in the year, in second grade, to launch the class, I might expect to find:

1. What is the difference of 9 and 5?

2. What number is the same as 5 tens and 7 tens?

3. What number is 10 less than 83?

4. Draw a four-sided figure and all of its diagonals.

5. About how long is this pencil in centimeters?

Quick, focused, aligned with the curriculum, reflective of what is coming on the Grade 3 State Test, and wonderfully informative. What more could we ask from the first few minutes of a lesson?

Or take an Algebra I class, about two-thirds of the way through the year, that starts, even before the bell rings, with the following four problems on the board:

1. What is the value of $3a - 6b$ when $a = -4$ and $b = -3$?

2. A line is defined by the function $g(x) = \frac{3}{2} x - 2$. What is the slope and what is the y-intercept of the line that represents this function?

3. The cost of a substance is directly proportional to its weight. If 30 grams of the substance costs \$45, what is the cost of 6 grams of the substance?

4. A population P increases by 5% each year for 2 years. Write an expression for the population in terms of P after 2 years.

This is a set of four straightforward problems that could just as easily be on the course final exam. They are four problems that every algebra student should be able to breeze through, but often can't. And they are four problems that clearly inform both you and your students whether or not they have broadly mastered these key aspects of algebra.

SO WHAT SHOULD WE SEE IN AN EFFECTIVE MATHEMATICS CLASSROOM?

- A deliberate and carefully planned reliance on ongoing, cumulative review of key skills and concepts
- Using cumulative review to keep skills and understandings fresh, reinforce previously taught material, and give students a chance to clarify their understandings
- Classes that waste no time and begin with substantive mathematics at the very start of every class
- The use of a brief review and whole-class checking of "mini-math" questions as an opportunity to re-teach when necessary

---

Accessible Mathematics

It's Not Hard to Figure Out Why Reading Works Better Than Math

3

INSTRUCTIONAL SHIFT 2
Adapt what we know works in our reading programs and apply it to mathematics instruction.

Consider a typical, not particularly exemplary, reading class using an equally typical basal reading program. The students encounter the sentence JANE WENT TO THE STORE. Listen to the sequence of questions that are commonly used to help these students develop reading comprehension skills:

- "Can you read the sentence aloud?"
- "Can you tell me where Jane went?"
- "Can you tell me who went to the store?"
- "Can you tell me why Jane might have gone to the store?"
- "Do you think it made sense for Jane to go to the store?"

Note the careful progression from literal to inferential to evaluative comprehension. Note that this progression is applied to *all* students; reading teachers would never stop after only the first three questions. Note that in reading instruction, we frequently ask students questions that do not have a single correct answer or answers that come literally from the text. And note that the last two questions are asked as frequently in a remedial class as in a class for the gifted. But most important, note how questions that demand inferential and evaluative comprehension dovetail with emerging brain research findings about how higher-order questions like this support the development of more and stronger neural connections in the brain. To be blunt, these are the questions that enable students to truly become smarter!

Consider the power of the "why" question to which it would not be surprising to hear "She needed cigarettes" or "They ran out of milk" or "They needed bread" or "She needed some new clothes." Then consider the thinking and reasoning that is stimulated by the reasonableness question, which elicits such answers as "Yes, they really needed milk for the breakfast cereal" or "No, she should quit smoking and she shouldn't leave the kids home alone in the first place."

Now compare this brief vignette about reading instruction with typical mathematics instruction. Consider how different the approaches used in math are—and how much narrower than what we've just seen in reading. As one example, envision the way a typical mathematics class often begins and listen in: "Take out your homework! Emily, your homework please. Good. Nice work. Tony? Missing again? Okay, here we go. Boys and girls, number one, answer 19. Any questions? I didn't think so. Great. Number two, 37.5. Okay? Number three, I got 186."

Look in the mirror and reflect on how yesterday's assignment of exercises 1–19 from page 244 gets translated today into 10 mindless, wasted minutes of "going over the homework." It is typically accomplished by reading answers that few students care about to exercises that even fewer care about. And then we wonder why there are problems! What else should we expect when the recitation of correct answers (essentially literal comprehension) is accompanied by little or no "Why?" "How did you get that?" "What do others think?" or "Is that reasonable?"—the very questions that elicit the mathematical analogies of inferential and evaluative comprehension in reading? Then consider how this narrow focus on the right answer is just as likely to be seen when going over homework as during core instruction of new content.

Just watch the students in a class when the homework is "gone over." Typically, if a few students are selected to put their work on the board, only that student and the teacher, squinting at the board, are able to decipher the student's calculations. It is just as typical that only the right answer is valued and that work is reviewed only in the case of an incorrect answer. But back to question 1. You've announced that the answer is 19, and maybe the board work confirms 19. Those students who got 19 just check it correct. Those who got it wrong will frequently—and very wisely—cross out their answer and replace it with 19.

That's why homework assignments with too many "practice" problems that cannot possibly all be reviewed the next day are so counterproductive. That's why fewer problems and more productive homework review enable us to focus on "Why?" "How did you get that?" "Who has a different way?" "What do others think?" and "Is that reasonable?"—exactly the questions successfully used to develop reading comprehension.

But all of mathematics instruction, not just homework review, benefits from examining the parallels to teaching reading. Once again, we're reminded that good math instruction, like the follow-up questions that extend literal comprehension in reading, *begins* with an answer. In effective instruction, you never stop when the same three students call out "19," so you can move on to the next question. Instead, we keep "Does that make sense?"—that is, "Do you comprehend?"—in the foreground at all times.

What sense does that make?

Obviously, moving beyond right answers, adapting what we know works better in reading than in math, and drawing from emerging brain research takes time. I hear again and again that there isn't enough time to build from answers, to seek alternative approaches, and to ensure student understanding. The answer is as simple as it is discomforting: less really is more! Racing through a jam-packed curriculum and a 700-page textbook is senseless if we know ahead of time that fewer than half are likely to succeed, especially if "success" might mean nothing more than superficial understanding demonstrated by good memorizers or effective listeners. It makes no sense to assign, as homework, thirty or forty practice problems that serve only as busy work and can't reasonably be reviewed in meaningful ways. And it makes no sense to try to cover so much material during a school year when every professional bone in your body tells you it's not sinking in for many, it's not making sense to many, and it's creating more and more serious long-term mathematics problems.

If you feel, however, that your students *must* have more practice each night, consider assignments where two-thirds of the problems

HW
2/3 old
1/3 current practice
for approaching
Proficiency

focus on previously studied material, and let students self-check their work on these problems. This enables you to keep the focus on the one-third of the assignment that needs to be reviewed in depth.

SO WHAT SHOULD WE SEE IN AN EFFECTIVE MATHEMATICS CLASSROOM?

- Consistent parallels are apparent between the types of questions that require inferential and evaluative comprehension in reading instruction and the probing for ways in which the answers were found, alternative approaches, and reasonableness in mathematics instruction.
- All numerical and one-word answers are consistently greeted with a request for justification.
- Only reasonable homework assignments are given, and when homework is reviewed, the focus is on explanation and understanding, not on checking for right answers.

Accessible Mathematics

Picture It, Draw It

4

INSTRUCTIONAL SHIFT 3
Use multiple representations of mathematical entities.

Without question, one of the most common responses I have when sitting in the back of a mathematics class is screaming under my breath, "Draw a picture!" or "Use a number line!" or "Ask them what it looks like!" The failure to capture the mathematics being taught with a picture that helps students visualize what is going on is one of the most serious missed opportunities I observe.

Here's the monologue I often use to help teachers, administrators, and parents understand the importance of pictorial representations and the power of visualizing mathematical entities. "Ready, set, in your mind's eye I would like you to picture three quarters. That's all, three quarters. Okay? Now, please erase that picture and create a second, different picture of three quarters. Ready to see what we've come up with? Great! Let's see. How many saw 25 cents, 25 cents, and 25 cents—that is, money or coins in the form of three quarters? Raise your hands if that is one of the ways you saw three quarters. Look at all the hands. Thank goodness for money. Okay, let's see what else we have. How many of you saw three over four in its abstract splendor? Interesting, that's not as many hands as for money. Now, how many of you saw pizza pies or apple pies or window panes with three of the four pieces or sections shaded? It seems that most of you now have most of your representations on the table. So now it gets interesting. How many of you saw four octopuses or four beach balls or four objects and three of them were a different color or striped? Look around the room, there aren't a lot of hands." Do you know why multiplication and division of fractions is such a nightmare for kids? It's because neither teachers nor students recognize that pizza pie and fractional parts of wholes just aren't always as strong a representation for multiplication and division of fractions as fractional parts of sets. In other words, *seeing* that 10 people can be served when we have 5 pizza pies and each person eats $\frac{1}{2}$ a pie—a set of 5 rather than 5 parts of a whole—supports student understanding of why $5 \div \frac{1}{2}$ is 10, as well as giving meaning to division by fractions. In fact, without a picture, all we provide our students is a rule about inverting and multiplying that is quickly forgotten, is misused, or just doesn't help a lot of them. But we're not done. "How many of you saw a number line—here's zero and here's one, so three-quarters is sitting here closer to the one? Look at that. How many saw a ruler—here's the zero, here's an inch and you saw the little tick mark representing three-quarters of an inch? And finally, did anyone bake last night? Who saw a measuring cup and it was three-quarters full?"

To hammer home this point, I often follow up with "Okay, so quickly now, tell me what the sum of $2\frac{1}{2}$ and $1\frac{3}{4}$ is. Rarely does an answer get called out quickly. This isn't surprising since most people are struggling to put the $1\frac{3}{4}$ under the $2\frac{1}{2}$ and then insert a pair of equals signs to get two mixed numbers with a common denominator of four. That's the rule. That's the way we're supposed to do the math, and that's the way that leaves far too many students up the creek without a paddle. Forget about $2\frac{1}{2}$ and $1\frac{3}{4}$ for a moment and think about $2.50 and $1.75. It is very common for people to add $2 to $2.50, get $4.50 and then subtract $0.25 to get $4.25, or four and a quarter. Or think about $2\frac{1}{2}$ inches and $1\frac{3}{4}$ inches on a ruler, where it is natural to add 2 inches to $2\frac{1}{2}$ inches and then move back $\frac{1}{4}$ inch.

Why bother? Because we won't help make mathematics work for a much larger proportion of the student body until and unless we recognize that abstractions like $\frac{3}{4}$ or rules for dividing fractions

Accessible Mathematics

work fine for some students but *must* be grounded in pictures and models for others. Consider the common teaching experience of working with four fifth graders. We're adding mixed numbers, and to help these students, we encourage them to "think money." Money works for Cheryl, it works for Hector, and it even works for Cherita. You're feeling great. Money always worked for you when doing fractions, and it's a strategy that has served you well working with students. But then there's Maria, who responds, "What do you mean by money? I don't get this!" If we're honest with ourselves, it's almost impossible not to get frustrated with Maria. It's almost impossible not to communicate in what may be not-so-subtle ways that we think Maria has a problem. But it's not Maria's problem. It's not her fault that money is not a dominant or particularly helpful representation for her. Instead of the "money hint," all Maria needs is a "think ruler" or "think measuring cup" hint. Only then is Maria likely to say, "Well, why didn't you tell me to use a measuring cup? I have 2 and a half cups of flour and 1 and three-quarters cups more, for a total of four and one-quarter cups. That's easy!"

The simple reality every teacher faces in a class of twenty-five students is that very rarely do more than half of the students process the math being taught, see the math being taught, or feel the math being taught in the same way their teacher is seeing it. Chances are we're seeing a set of fractions on a number line to determine their order, while our students just see a set of numbers separated by bars. We might translate two integers to a thermometer to help us visualize why $-15 + 25$ is 10, while our students are struggling with the concept of absolute value and the rule for adding integers. Without even realizing it, we are seeing a line with positive slope on a coordinate grid, while our students can only resort to $f(x) = 3x - 7$. That's why our presentations and our explanations need to be rich with multiple representations, and that's why we need to rely on our students to put forth their thinking and describe the various ways they are visualizing the mathematics.

Or consider what can happen when we encounter an almost meaningless "20 centimeters" in a word problem we've presented and ask, "Show me with your fingers 20 centimeters." First we get an immediate sense of how many of our students have a rough sense of how long 20 centimeters is. But the real teaching and learning begins when we follow up with "Explain how you knew that the length you've shown is about 20 centimeters." Here's what can happen:

- "I knew that my pinky nail is about a centimeter, so I counted out 10 pinky nails and doubled the distance to get 20 centimeters."

- "I knew that my index finger is about a decimeter, or 10 centimeters, so I put my two index fingers together."

- "I remembered that a 12-inch ruler has 30 centimeters on the side opposite inches, so 20 centimeters is $\frac{2}{3}$ of the ruler, or about 8 inches."

- "I looked at Jim's hands and copied his length."

- "I knew that a meter is 100 centimeters and also about a yard. So I held my hands about 3 feet apart, chopped that in half, chopped that in half, and got a little smaller for 20 centimeters."

- "I knew from my ruler that there are about $2\frac{1}{2}$ centimeters in an inch, so 20 centimeters would be about 8 inches.

In this fashion, we are not only drawing out a range of alternative ways to estimate a length but also gathering important information on how our students are thinking and connecting measurement to their own lives. We see the power of asking, "How did you see it?" over and over again as we construct engaged communities of learners in our classrooms.

Or take the bar model that plays such a prominent role in the Singapore Math materials. Beginning in first grade, number facts or number bonds are represented by a simple part-part-whole bar like the one shown in Figure 4-1.

In addition to helping visualize $4 + 5 = 9$, $5 + 4 = 9$, $9 - 5 = 4$, and $9 - 4 = 5$ and how such fact families are related, the same bar model emerges naturally when students need to deal with something like how much money was spent if Jennifer leaves home with $14.98 and returns with only $5.43, as shown in Figure 4-2.

Figure 4-1

4	5

9

Figure 4-2

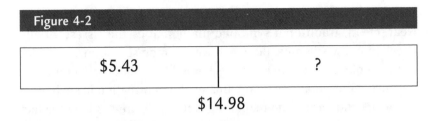

$5.43	?

$14.98

Students who struggle with deciding whether they need to add or subtract, or later to multiply or divide, find the organizing potential of the bar model incredibly helpful.

To see where such models or representations end up, consider the following typical "system of equations" word problem from algebra:

> Siti packs her clothes into a suitcase and it weighs 29 kg.
>
> Rahim packs his clothes into an identical suitcase and it weighs 11 kg.
>
> Siti's clothes are three times as heavy as Rahim's.
>
> What is the mass of Rahim's clothes?
>
> What is the mass of the suitcase?

For most students, there is only one way to solve such a problem:

> Identify your variables:
>
> Let S = the weight of Siti's clothes
> Let R = the weight of Rahim's clothes
> Let X = the weight of the suitcase
>
> Set up the appropriate equations:
>
> $S = 3R$
> $S + X = 29$
> $R + X = 11$
>
> Substituting $3R$ for S in the second equation results in $3R + X = 29$. Subtracting $R + X = 11$ from $3R + X = 29$ results in $2R = 18$, so R must equal 9.
> If $R = 9$ and we know that $R + X = 11$, then $X = 2$.

So the suitcase weighs 2 kilograms and the problem is solved. Neat, clean, traditional symbolic mathematics that is essentially Greek to many students. But when we use representations, variables can be replaced with areas, and expanded bar models are often very effective representations for organizing the information in such word problems and easing their solution. Note in Figure 4-3 how the fact that Siti's clothes are three times as heavy as Rahim's is simply represented by three congruent boxes for Siti and one such box for Rahim. We now know that the total weights of 11 kg for Rahim and 29 kg for Siti include the weight of the suitcase, so it becomes visually and immediately clear that Siti's 29 kg is made up of three "boxes" of clothes and one "box of suitcase," while Rahim's 11 kg is made up of one "box" of clothes and one "box of suitcase." Far clearer for many students than substituting variables and subtracting equations is the visual clarity of replacing one of Siti's "boxes" of clothes and her suitcase with 11 kg since, from Rahim, this is what we know they weigh. This leaves the two remaining "boxes" of Siti's clothes weighing (by subtraction) 18 kg, so each "box" must weigh 9 kg. Writing in 9's and the 2 for the suitcase results in all the necessary answers.

Look at how we transform our classroom dynamics with simple questions like "Can you show us?" and "Can you explain how you saw

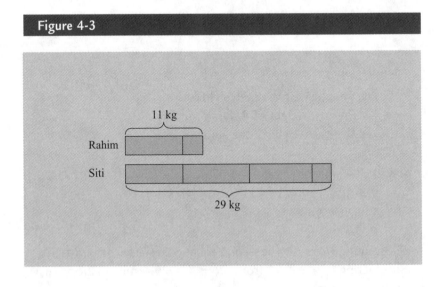

Figure 4-3

For an amazing website that shows how the bar model can be used to solve a range of problems, see www.thesingaporemaths.com.

it?" Look at how they contribute to a true community of learners. The so-called brighter students can inform the so-called weaker students, and the so-called weaker students can draw on their natural sense of mathematics to inform the so-called brighter students. And look at how this valuing of alternative approaches enriches our instruction and provides new levels of access to mathematical understanding.

So think about mathematics classes that consistently provide opportunities for students to draw, to describe, to model, and to visualize the mathematics they are learning. Think about standard operating classroom procedure including such activities as:

- Show me that area (about 10 square inches) with your fingers. Now show me 10 inches square. How much larger is the second figure?
- Draw three different pictures of $2\frac{3}{4}$.
- Show me where 3π lives on the number line. How did you think that out?
- Picture the decimal 1.2. Describe your picture. Now create a second, different picture of 1.2.
- Ready. Draw and label an isosceles right triangle. How do you know your triangle is both right and isosceles?
- If your left index fingertip is the origin, use your right hand to trace the line $y = -3x - 5$.

SO WHAT SHOULD WE SEE IN AN EFFECTIVE MATHEMATICS CLASSROOM?

- Frequent use of pictorial representations to help students visualize the mathematics they are learning
- Frequent use of the number line and bar models to represent numbers and word problems
- Frequent opportunities for students to draw or show and then describe what is drawn or shown

---

Language-Rich Classes

5

Create language-rich classroom routines.

I'm reminded of how important a command of language is to learning and how important an ongoing bombardment of language is to literacy every time I wander through my local Whole Foods. For almost 30 years, I have been the food shopper in whatever family I've been a part of. I love food shopping, and I love observing other shoppers and the contents of their carts. Now that I've become the cook, as well as the shopper, and now that my local Whole Foods just happens to be in the rapidly gentrifying Logan Circle neighborhood of Washington, D.C., the food shopping experience is even more interesting. Do I want the fresh cilantro or just the organic parsley? Should I blacken the fresh Atlantic salmon with white pepper and cayenne or save time and money by just buying the store's blackened salmon filets?

But the real fun is listening in on the mother-child conversations as I wander up and down the aisles. Overwhelmingly we're talking about upper-middle-class D.C. professionals in their late thirties and early forties with their later-in-life infants. "I think we're going to get the organic pasta today. Here's the rigatoni. No, maybe the penne is a better idea." They're not chatting on their cell phone. They're not talking to themselves. They're just babbling to this little toddler head in a Snugli. I've actually heard moms discussing aloud the choice between the Bigalow tea "that Daddy likes and that comes in rectangular boxes" and the Republic of Tea "that Mommy likes and that comes in these cool cylinders." I've listened in as "bulbs of fennel," "spears of asparagus," and "sprigs of broccoli" are comically announced and deposited into the cart. It's obvious how lucky these kids are. They are immersed, from a very early age, in a language-rich world of context-based vocabulary. They are being given a head start on learning and, based on the emerging brain research, strengthening neural connections that directly affect the capacity to learn.

Look at how easily this translates into mathematics instruction. The problem we're solving in class involves the numbers 73 and 63. We put the numbers on the board and announce, "Tell the person next to you five things you see on the board." Here are some of the responses that have emerged in demonstration classes:

- Two odd numbers
- Two 2-digit numbers
- Two numbers 10 apart
- Three unique digits
- My grandparents
- The high and low temperatures
- One prime and one composite number
- A take-away-10 pattern
- My last two math test grades
- A sum of 136
- Threes in the ones place of both numbers

Now consider the questions and discussion that ensued from this "brain dump" when we followed up with such statements or questions as

- Convince me that they are both odd numbers. ("They both end in an odd number," "Neither can be divided evenly by 2," "Even numbers end in 0, 2, 4, 6, or 8, so these must both be odd.")

- How do you know they're 10 apart? ("Count up: 64, 65, 66, …," "If you subtract them, the difference is 10," "You can add 10 to 63 to get 73, so they're 10 apart," "63 lives upstairs from the 73 on the hundreds chart," "The units digits are the same, and the tens digits are one apart.")

- If the numbers represent Amanda's grandparents, what is the attribute ("age") and what is the unit ("years")?

- Convince me that there are two numbers ("63 and 73—two numbers that each have two digits"). Convince me that there are three numbers ("7, 6, and 3—the three unique digits"). Convince me that there are four numbers ("7, 3, 6, and 3—the four digits that make up the two numbers").

- Which number is prime and which is composite? How do you know? What are the factors of the prime number? What are the factors of the composite number?

- If they are indeed your last two math test scores, what is the mean of these grades?

Just look at the vocabulary that arises for the initial brain dump and the follow-up questions: *odd, numbers, digits, pattern, sum, difference, prime, composite,* and *mean.* Look at how these terms are used naturally and again and again in everyday classroom discourse when we strive to build language-rich classrooms.

By the way, the 63 and the 73 aren't test scores or grandparents, they're basketball game scores. The original problem from which the numbers were extracted is

> In a rough-and-tumble basketball game where you can score one point on foul shots, two points on baskets and three points on long three-point-range baskets, the score was tied 63 to 63 with three minutes left to play. The Owls went on a 10-to-0 run and beat the Vultures 73 to 63. In how many different ways could the Owls have scored these 10 unanswered points?

As soon as the class agrees, via a table or an organized list, that there are 14 different ways for the Owls to have scored 10 points, I "admit" to a reading error and indicate that, in fact, the Owls went on a 12–0 run and won the game 75 to 63. *Now* how many ways could they have scored these points?

Why bother? First, because so often students' problems arise *not* from a lack of mathematical understanding but from serious confusion with the English—that is, the terms and the vocabulary. And second, because the United States is increasingly non-English, and we've known for years that language-rich classrooms are the best vehicles for helping English language learners to prosper. We know how young children struggle with left and right and how older students confuse area and perimeter even when they understand the concepts. Think about the confusion that arises from the simple dot on a paper. It's just a *dot* when it's not in context, but the dot becomes a *period* when it happens to be placed at the end of a sentence and a *decimal point* when it happens to fit in between two digits. It is neither simple nor automatic to distinguish among these different names for the same object. Or think back to geometry class where we were bombarded with sentences like "The projection of a leg onto the hypotenuse of a right triangle is the mean proportion between the entire hypotenuse and the length of the projection of the leg onto the hypotenuse." What a mouthful and what a nightmare for most students to grasp even when the terms are clear, let alone when students are struggling with *hypotenuse, leg, projection,* and *mean proportion.* For a third grader whose native language is not English, a phrase like "write two 2-digit numbers on your paper" is not immediately obvious, and we need to recognize that the problem a student might have with this is just as likely to be a language problem as a mathematics problem.

Or look at what happens when we encounter $2\frac{1}{4}$ in a problem. Just write $2\frac{1}{4}$ on the board in a fifth-, sixth- or seventh-grade class and ask your students to tell their partner three things they see on the board. Perhaps with a little prodding or encouragement, what is likely to emerge is another "brain dump" that needs to be written on the board:

- A mixed number
- A whole number
- A fraction
- 2.25
- $2\frac{2}{8}$
- 2.250
- $\frac{9}{4}$
- An arrow just to the right of 2 on the number line

Once the list has been generated, it's time to follow up with questions like

- What makes this a mixed number?
- Why is 2.25 equivalent to $2\frac{1}{4}$?

- Can you name another decimal equivalent?
- What do we call $\frac{9}{4}$?
- Why is $\frac{9}{4}$ equivalent to $2\frac{1}{4}$?
- Which number is the numerator? The denominator?

In this fashion, we present, review, and/or reinforce nearly all of the critical vocabulary attached to fractions and fraction equivalents. We can then add a poster to our word wall that keeps these terms front and center in our classrooms for the rest of the year.

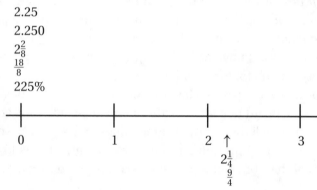

I observed a middle school class where students were greeted with 2 : 5 on the board. The class had just begun to work with ratios and the teacher asked, "What do you see?" After quickly gathering such answers as "a ratio," "two numbers separated by a colon," "two equal parts of one thing for five equal parts of another thing," the teacher added the words *walkers* and *bus riders* under the 2 and 5, respectively. She then asked the students to write three different sentences that are based on those data. In the process the ratio was reversed ("there are five bus riders for every two walkers") and related to fractions ("$\frac{2}{7}$ of these students walk"). This simple introduction opened the door to how fractions and ratios are related, part-to-part relationships, and part-to-whole relationships. Finally, she asked, "If there are 28 students, how many walk and how many take the bus?" and "If there are 150 walkers, how many bus

Accessible Mathematics

riders must there be?" In 6 minutes this class was bombarded by language and key mathematical concepts all embedded in an open-ended exploration of a simple ratio.

I was at a high school recently and watched in amazement as, halfway through the lesson, the teacher wrote $f(x) = x^2 - 3x + 5$ on the board and said to her students, "Tell the person sitting next to you three things you see." After about a minute she then said, "Tell me what you saw" and, collecting their responses, wrote the following on the board:

- A function
- A quadratic
- Coefficients
- Three terms
- A constant
- A trinomial
- A linear term
- A second-degree polynomial
- An equals sign
- A U-shaped curve that opens upward
- A parabola
- Two roots

This list encompasses a significant proportion of the critical terms and understandings for the quadratic functions unit of Algebra I or II. Without a familiarity with these terms and what they mean, student access to algebra is significantly limited. With an ongoing focus on the terms and language of algebra, they become commonplace and gradually internalized.

Of course, the heavy lifting occurs *after* the list is generated, as the discussion builds from the list and turns to things like

- Which is the constant? What does it do to the function?
- What makes it a trinomial?
- How many coefficients does the equation have?
- What makes it a quadratic?
- What makes it a function?
- How do you know it opens upward?
- What's a parabola?

In sum, we well know that in order to demonstrate proficient mathematical understanding on state tests, students require language skills. We also know that one of the simplest and easiest ways to take the students who are just below proficient and move them to proficient is to attend to the fact that they just may not have known five mathematical terms. In other words, like all languages, mathematics must be encountered orally and in writing. Like all vocabulary, mathematical terms must be used again and again in context and linked to more familiar words until they become internalized. For example:

> Perimeter is border.
> Area is covering.
> Circumference is the pizza crust or your belt.
> Quotient is sharing.
> A centimeter is about a pinky fingernail.
> A milligram is about a grain of sand.
> A liter is about a quart.
> A cylinder is a can.
> A prism is a box.
> Average or mean is typical.

Even as adults we know that we rely on such connections, and sometimes even on mnemonics, to help us make sense of the mathematics we use. For example, I can never remember whether a 3×4 matrix has three rows and four columns or three columns and four rows. So I rely on RC Cola and remember that RC, or Row then Column, means that an $a \times \mathbf{b}$ matrix has a rows and $\mathbf{b}$ columns!

Or think about the language-based memory device that many adults tell me they rely on to remember that 7 times 8 is 56. They recount how their fifth-grade teacher told them to think: "five, six, seven, eight" so 7×8 comes from 5, 6 or 56!

SO WHAT SHOULD WE SEE IN AN EFFECTIVE MATHEMATICS CLASSROOM?

- An ongoing emphasis on the use and meaning of mathematical terms, including their definitions and their connections to real-world entities and/or pictures
- Student and teacher explanations that make frequent and precise use of mathematics terms, vocabulary, and notation
- An extensive use of word walls that capture the key terms and vocabulary with pictures when appropriate and in English as well as Spanish when appropriate

Building Number Sense

6

INSTRUCTIONAL SHIFT 5

Take every available opportunity to support the development of number sense.

Here is a typical test item: Tom has $10.00. Sandwiches cost $1.89 each. What is the greatest number of sandwiches that Tom can buy?

    a. 5
    b. 8
    c. 11
    d. 18

This multiple-choice item is clearly designed to assess a student's ability to identify the correct operation to solve a simple one-step word problem and, in this case, correctly find a quotient. Note that to best assess this objective, the distracters represent, in rounded form, the quotient, difference, sum, and product of the two numbers in the problem. Note too that an ounce of number sense—at $2 each, I can buy only 5 sandwiches—is all that is needed to answer the problem correctly.

We know that this is exactly how our brightest students solve this problem. We know that this is also exactly how our wealthiest students are taught to think by Kaplan and other test prep operations.

And we know that our weakest students too often foolishly struggle with finding the quotient of 1.89 divided by 10 to answer this item. That's one reason why number sense and explicitly teaching number sense and fostering its development in all students is so important.

Number sense—a comfort with numbers that includes estimation, mental math, numerical equivalents, a use of referents like $\frac{1}{2}$ and 50%, a sense of order and magnitude, and a well-developed understanding of place value—is one of the overarching goals of mathematics learning. It follows that instruction resulting in the development of number sense must be an ongoing feature of all instruction. One strategy for accomplishing this is to pause frequently and, regardless of the specific mathematical topic being taught, ask such questions as

- Which is most or greatest? How do you know?
- Which is least or smallest? How do you know?
- What else can you tell me about those numbers?
- How else can we express that number? Is there still another way?
- About how much would that be? How did you get that?

More specifically:

- Given a problem with 1534, 4933, and 588, you can ask: Which is the greatest and which is least? About how much is the sum? How did you get that? Which number is different from the other two? In what ways?

- Given a table with $2\frac{1}{2}$, 5, and $\frac{11}{2}$, you can ask the same questions and then ask: What's the sum? What's the difference between the greatest and least? How else can you express $\frac{11}{2}$ and how do you know and what do you call those numbers? ($5\frac{1}{2}$, 5.5, $\frac{22}{4}$, 5.50, etc.)

- Given the number 0.2, you can ask: How else can you express that? ($\frac{2}{10}$, $\frac{1}{5}$, 20%, .20)

- Given a problem with 57 and 67, pause and ask, as we've seen in the previous chapter, "What do you see?" in the hope of eliciting such statements as
  - Two 2-digit numbers
  - Two odd numbers
  - A sum of 144

- A difference of 10
- Two numbers with the same digit in the ones place
- One prime and one composite number

- Given a page of subtraction exercises like 1539 – 612 or percent exercises like 15% of $26.75, ask students for a reasonable estimate and a justification and encourage multiple reasonable estimates and alternative approaches.

Let's focus on place value. Too often place value is relegated to Chapter 1 and the first couple of weeks of school. Too often place value is limited to such insipid and unnatural questions as "What is the value of the 8 in 4289?" and "What digit is the hundredths place of 4.2958?" Given the important of place value for understanding computational algorithms and for effectively estimating, there is an urgent need for us to go beyond this superficiality and develop a mature sense of place value in all students. Instead of limiting place value to digits and places, we need to ask the important questions over and over again:

- About how much is that?
- What's 10 or 100 or 1000 or one-tenth or one-hundredth more or less?
- What's 10 or 100 or 1000 times as much as that number or one-tenth or one-hundredth of that number?

For example:

- Given the number 475,493 that emerges from a problem the class is working on, look what can happen when you ask, "About how much is that and where did your approximation come from?"
  - About 475, 000; I rounded to the nearest thousand.
  - About 475,500; I rounded to the nearest hundred.
  - About a half a million; I rounded up to the nearest hundred thousand.
- Given the number 25.925, consider asking the following questions:
  - On the number line, is this to the left or right of 25? Is it closer to 25 or 26? Why?
  - What's a tenth less than this number? How did you get that?

Accessible Mathematics

- What's a tenth more than this number?
- What's a hundredth less?
- What's a thousand times this number?

In fact, every number that emerges during a math class presents a golden opportunity to strengthen number sense. I've been known to announce that as of this morning my age is 28,935,285 and then ask students to guess what the unit of time must be. Is it days? Hours? Minutes? Seconds? Starting with a guess that I'm, say, 53 *years* old produces the following:

53 years
53×365.25 days/year $= 19,358.25$ days
$19,358.25 \times 24$ hours/day $= 464,598$ hours
$464,598 \times 60$ minutes/hour $= 27,875,880$ minutes
$27,875,880 \times 60$ seconds/minute $= 1,672,552,800$ seconds

And then the fun (and the real teaching) begins with questions and the ensuing discussion:

- So what is the correct unit for the 28,935,285 that represents my actual age? How do you know? Could it be seconds? (Answer: Not unless I'm only about 1 year old!)

- So about how many days old *is* a 53-year-old? If we say about 19,000, to what place did we round this number? (To the nearest thousand) Could we say about 20,000 days? (Yes, we rounded to the nearest ten thousand.)

- How many hours old will this 53-year-old be in another 100,000 hours? How many hours old was this person 10,000 hours ago? How do you know?

- So if I'm older than 53, then how old am I? How can we figure this out based on a 53-year-old being 27,875,880 minutes old and me being 28,935,285 minutes old?

- And if, as of this morning, I'm 28,935,285 minutes old, can you figure out when is my birthday?

- Finally (or on the next test): Suppose the principal [?]
  class and announces that she is exactly one million [?]
  her claim reasonable or not? Explain why.

In other words, mathematics instruction that emerges [?] triguing claim about me (my age in minutes) takes us to m[?] time units and conversions, place value, and rounding [?] bers; and ends with a summary task that is built from an[?] and tells us whether our students have in fact learned what was expected.

SO WHAT SHOULD WE SEE IN AN EFFECTIVE MATHEMATICS CLASSROOM?

- An unrelenting focus on estimation and justifying estimates to computations and to the solution of problems
- An unrelenting focus on a mature sense of place value
- Frequent discussion and modeling about how to use number sense to "outsmart" the problem
- Frequent opportunities to put the calculator aside and estimate or compute mentally when appropriate

---

Accessible Mathematics

Milking the Data

7

Build from graphs, charts, and tables.

Here's a perfect example of missed opportunities. We're in Chapter 1. It's early in the year and we're still establishing classroom norms and routines. We're on the lesson that comes after place value to millions and now focuses on ordering and comparing large numbers. Our textbook has the following table in the exercise set:

Ticket Sales for Classical Music Concerts	
Concert	**Tickets Sold**
Beethoven	385,204
Mozart	259,593
Haydn	285,447
Chopin	327,982

Although this exercise is based on an absurd context and utterly divorced from our students' frames of reference, we follow along with the script and ask, from the textbook, "Which concert has the greatest number of tickets sold?" That's it. Four luscious 6-digit numbers and four incredible composers, and all we ask for is the largest of the four numbers.

Consider instead employing the "So?" strategy and asking pairs of students what questions arise from the data. In this manner, we not only engage students in their own problem formulation but also gather a set of questions that rescue the four sets of classical music concert ticket sales. Here is what is likely to emerge in a class where this approach has been routinized into the culture:

- About how many tickets were sold altogether?
- Which concert was probably the least popular?
- Did they reach their goal of 1 million tickets?
- About how many more tickets were sold for Beethoven than for Chopin?
- Which concert sold closest to 300,000 tickets?
- About how many more tickets were sold to the most popular concert than to the least popular concert? What percent more tickets was this?

Such a set of questions milks the data for more than one simple exercise and reinforces many aspects of the number sense curriculum. Imagine the discussion as each question is answered and justified and as students' abilities to draw and justify conclusions from data are developed.

Or consider just putting the data on the board and asking students what the data might represent.

385,204
259,593
285,447
327,982

Instead of providing the context, exploit the power of asking students to make inferences about four such 6-digit numbers. Consider students working in pairs, proposing a context, and letting the class judge its reasonableness or appropriateness. One might hear:

- The populations of four cities
- The amount of money four rich families earn in a year
- The area, in square kilometers, of four small countries

- The total seasonal attendance at the home basketball games for a college team
- The number of miles traveled by four space shuttle missions

What we know is that many real-world applications of mathematics (and hence many test items) arise from the data presented in graphs, charts, and tables. To best prepare students to make sense of data and draw conclusions from data, as well as to reinforce skills, we should "milk" the graphs, tables, and charts that abound. Given a graph or a table, we can ask students to identify and justify three possible conclusions that could be drawn from the data presented. We can ask students to open their textbooks or a newspaper and go on a data scavenger hunt in search of a bar graph, a number between 100,000 and 500,000, a graph with an interrupted scale, or a table where the largest number is more than twice the smallest number.

Here are four examples to emphasize how starting with a set of intriguing data opens the floodgates to exactly the kind of instruction we have been discussing. That is, to instruction that incorporates systematic ongoing review, instruction that focuses on the development of number sense, and instruction that supports a language-rich classroom.

Example 1

Asia	16,988,000
Africa	11,506,000
North America	9,390,000
South America	6,795,000
Antarctica	5,500,000
Europe	3,745,000
Australia	2,968,000

In addition to asking "What questions and conclusions arise from the data?" to get things started, these data lend themselves to such questions as:

- What is the most likely unit for the seven numbers? (square miles)
- About how many square miles of land are on the earth? Is this more or less than half the surface area of the planet?

- About how many Europes are needed to cover Asia?
- How then can we add population data to see which continents are most crowded?
- About how much bigger is the largest continent than the smallest continent?

This last question is critically important for differentiating absolute change (Asia is about 14,000,000 square miles larger than Australia) that results from subtraction and relative change (Asia is about 5 times larger than Australia) that results from division.

I have also seen teachers present tabular data like these on an overhead projector, using paper to create windows that reveal the data a little piece at a time. For example, students first might see only 6,795,000 and be asked about how much this is. Then the numbers above and below might be revealed, leading to a discussion of largest and smallest or differences. At this point the teacher might reveal the entire right-hand column of numbers and ask what they might represent. Students are likely to suggest populations or dollar amounts. At this point, revealing only South America from the left-hand column opens the doors to powerful interdisciplinary instruction as students wrestle with the size of continents.

Example 2

Weeks	Roger	Jamie	Rhonda
0	210	154	113
2	202	150	108
4	196	146	105

Here's a case in which the first question ought to be "What is the story here?" to stimulate inferential reasoning about the context that leads to a range of possibilities, including three people on diets, in which case the unit for the nine 3-digit numbers is probably pounds. When asked to create questions for these data, students are likely to come up with:

- At these rates, what will each person probably weigh after 6 and 8 weeks on the diet?

Accessible Mathematics

- Which person is doing best after 4 weeks?
- Which dieter is probably being the smartest?

The discussion that emerges is likely to include such conclusions as

- Roger is doing best because he has lost the most weight (14 pounds), but if he's normal he's likely to weigh 200 after 6 weeks because he goes on a binge and gains a lot of it back!

- Jaime is doing best because she has been consistent (losing 4 pounds every 2 weeks), but healthy dieters tend to lose a little less each week, and at this rate Jamie will disappear entirely in 38 weeks!

- Rhonda is doing best because she has lost the greatest percentage of her weight (8 out of 113 is 7%), but chances are that someone as small as Rhonda shouldn't be dieting in the first place and may even have an eating disorder.

Note the existence of more than one correct answer and the importance of justification for any answer provided. Note too the nuanced reality that there are often many correct ways to interpret data. And note the thinking and reasoning that emerge from such data and the accompanying questions.

Example 3

The local pizza restaurant sells a medium-sized, 8-slice, 12-inch-diameter cheese pizza for $8.99. Additional toppings are $0.75 each. Design and describe the characteristics of an extra large pizza at this restaurant.

In your description, be sure to include *and justify* all of the following:
- the shape and dimensions of the extra large pizza
- the number of slices into which the pizza will be cut
- how the pizza will be sliced
- the price of the pizza
- the cost of each topping

In this situation, students have the opportunity to design a pizza and base their pricing and sizing decisions on a set of information given for the medium-sized pizza. The task entails measurement, proportional reasoning, and even some geometry. Thus it is an ideal Friday and weekend task to reinforce a broad range of mathematics skills (and to encourage visiting a pizza emporium to conduct some "research").

Example 4

The data in the table below are drawn from the Federal Highway Administration.

Increasingly Crowded Roads in the United States		
	1996	**Growth since 1970**
Miles driven	2.5 billion	123%
Number of vehicles	206.4 million	90%
Number of drivers	179.5 million	61%
Population	265.3 million	30%
Miles of roads	3.9 million	7%

a. Use the data in the table to estimate the number of miles driven, the number of vehicles, the number of drivers, the population, and the number of miles of roads in 1970.
b. Use the data in the table to calculate the change in the number of cars per mile of road between 1970 and 1996, and use your result to answer the following question: Why are roads more crowded?
c. There is an error in one of the five pieces of data in the 1996 column of the table. Identify which number must be wrong, explain why this must be the case, and propose a correction.

Once again this task is based on data, and once again it expands quickly to a range of mathematical skills and concepts, including the critical opportunity to "debug" the situation by identifying the error. (If 206 million vehicles travel a total of 2.5 billion miles, each vehicle is going only about 10 miles a year. Because the average vehicle travels closer to 10,000 miles per year, we would assume that the top bar should be labeled 2.5 *trillion* miles!)

SO WHAT SHOULD WE SEE IN AN EFFECTIVE MATHEMATICS CLASSROOM?

- An abundance of problems drawn from the data presented in tables, charts, and graphs
- Opportunities for students to make conjectures and draw conclusions from data presented in tables, charts, and graphs
- Frequent conversion, with and without technology, of data in tables and charts into various types of graphs, with discussions of their advantages, disadvantages, and appropriateness

How Big, How Far, How Much?

8

INSTRUCTIONAL SHIFT 7

Tie the math to such questions as How big? How much? How far? to increase the natural use of measurement throughout the curriculum.

No strand in the curriculum is consistently as weak as measurement, and no chapter is more consistently skipped or raced through than the one on measurement. Whether it is TIMSS international data, NAEP national data, or state test results, measurement in general and student performance on measurement tasks are embarrassingly weak. Perhaps it's because measurement is so often the first chapter to be skipped in order to focus on computation. Perhaps it's because the need to address both customary *and* metric systems adds a significant burden to how measurement must be taught in the United States. Perhaps it's because the science-like activities that are the best format for teaching and learning measurement are still so atypical after second or third grade. But just ask science teachers about their most serious concerns with the mathematics curriculum, and you hear that "the kids can't measure." In the face of these realities and in recognition of how pervasive measurement is in our lives, the alternative is to make measurement an ongoing part of daily instruction and the entry point for a larger chunk of the curriculum.

As we have seen again and again, we have a choice. We can walk the straight and narrow, teach by telling, teach the way most of us were taught, and leave far too many students without the mathematical preparation they so desperately need. Here is an all-too-familiar glimpse of such instruction as played out in a grade 7 or grade 10 measurement lesson:

"Good morning, boys and girls. Today's objective is to find the surface area of right circular cylinders." (You're following the teacher evaluation protocol and publicly stating the learning objective for the day. Unfortunately, in mathematics, stating the learning objective is often the best way to lose half of your class in the first few minutes. You know they're thinking something like "Not another stupid formula to memorize," but you forge ahead anyway.) "Please open your books to page 384 and look at Example 1." (Every math teacher knows that Example 1 provides a picture of the prototypical right circular cylinder with an integral height of 6 and an integral diameter of 4 next to the bold-faced formula **S.A. $= 2\pi rh + 2\pi r^2$.**) "Let's find the surface area of this figure."

But look at all that is missing:

- a can of soup or a barrel of hazardous waste that must be stored, to give the situation some meaningful context
- some measurement units, such as inches or meters, to add to the reality of the situation and to reinforce critical measurement understandings
- an estimate of the surface area
- attention to why the formula works and where it comes from
- attention to π, r, h, and ^{2}, the critical elements of the formula.

Instead, this typical lesson's primary focus is merely memorizing a formula whose derivation isn't addressed and plugging numbers for the radius and the height of imaginary cylinders into the formula to arrive at answers that are as meaningless as the unit-less measures of the radius and the height in the first place.

So this is where we confront the fundamental challenge that was addressed in Chapter 1: acknowledging the realities and problems with traditional practices and the dire need to teach in distinctly different ways from how we were taught. This is where we might turn to an alternative instructional script that begins to make measurement specifically—and mathematics generally—far more real, far more accessible, and far more effective.

"Good morning, my bright-eyed, bushytailed seventh graders," we might announce. "You're in luck! Today we get to work on one of my favorite problems. You've heard me talk about my son Ethan. Well, when Ethan was sixteen he cut his foot very badly and was bleeding all over the place. So we raced to the emergency room with his foot all wrapped up in gauze and towels. A few minutes later he's being stitched up and I'm stuck in the waiting room when all of a sudden the sirens start blaring and two nurses run to the ER admissions door. I hear one of the nurses exclaim, 'Oh, dear, this is serious. This next patient is completely burned.' The second nurse calmly advises: 'Don't worry. He's an adult so let's just order up 1000 square inches of skin from the skin graft bank.' So here are the data I have:

- adult male
- completely burned
- 1000 square inches of skin

It occurred to me, being the math nerd I proudly am, that there were really only two possible responses. Either I could relax with an 'Oh, good' after realizing that an adult does in fact have about 1000 square inches of skin, OR I could really get worried with an 'Oh, dear' after realizing that 1000 square inches is either not nearly enough or much too much. Fair enough? Any questions?"

In this manner, with a personal story, I have launched the lesson with a complex, thought-provoking problem. The questions that emerge usually focus on the patient ("Did he die?" "How big was he?") and open the door to the four-part task at hand:

In your groups of four, please answer the following four questions or tasks:

- Which response, "Oh, good" or "Oh, dear," is more appropriate?
- Explain your reasoning.
- Assuming you are the patient, how much skin would you hope was ordered up?
- Show how you arrived at your answer and be prepared to defend it to the class.

It is wonderful to wander around a classroom of interested students thoroughly engaged in the task of judging the reasonableness of ordering 1000 square inches of skin. It is a joy to watch the diverse styles and different approaches as students struggle with the novelty of the situation while knowing the task is as accessible as it is novel.

I often bring the class back together with three questions:

- Why did you care?
- What math did you use?
- Is there enough skin? That is, which expression ("Oh, good" or "Oh, dear") is most appropriate?

You know you've got them when they tell you, "I care because it could have been me" or "I care because I had to work with my partners" or "I care because I never thought about how much skin I have" or "I care because, I don't know, I mean I don't want to be burned." In short, they care because it's relevant, because we've piqued their curiosity, and because they can personalize the situation. Next, we list the estimation, the measurement, the multiplication, the conversion of units, the area, and the use of formulas that students claim to have used.

Finally, when the overwhelming majority of the class tells you "Oh, dear!"—that is, the patient is in trouble—I only have to say, "Convince me" to get an array of answers like these:

- "We thought we could use a paint roller and paint the front of your body. Then when you walk into the wall, we could measure the paint splat. We estimate that it is about 70 inches high and 18 inches wide, so that's more than 1000 already and we haven't painted your back, so there's no way that 1000 is enough."

- "We thought that the body is sort of like a tall box with dimensions 6 feet high by 1 foot wide by 1 foot deep. Counting the top and bottom, that's 26 square feet of area, or almost 4000 square inches."

- "We started with our thumbs, which are about 1 square inch, and counted on our chests, but then we realized that our thumb was too small. So we switched to our hands, which are about 6 inches $\times$ 4 inches so we figured 25 square inches for each hand print, or 100 square inches for each 4 handprints. We got close to 1000 square inches just for the skin between our necks and our waists."

- "We thought that 1000 square inches would be a square towel about 32 inches per side, and we didn't think a towel that small would come close to covering our whole bodies."

- "We also started with the 1000 square inches and thought that it would be the same size as a sheet of paper towel 10 inches wide and 100 inches, or 8 feet, long. If it takes 3 feet to wrap around a body, we'd only have three 10-inch wraps, and that's not enough."

- "We remembered that you always say that 'all measurement is referential,' so we took an $8\frac{1}{2} \times 11$ sheet of paper and figured that it was about 100 square inches. We wrapped it around our arms and then our legs and used up 1000 square inches before we got to our torso."

- "We thought that our bodies were cylinders or like the cardboard inside paper towel rolls. We figured that an adult was about 70 inches tall and about 36 inches around for a total of more than 2000 square inches."

Just look at what can happen when we provide engaging, complex tasks. Look at the richness that emerges when we empower students to do real thinking and reasoning. And look at how the concepts of area, surface area, and estimation emerge naturally. And now look at how the last student's answer has set the scene for you to ask: What happens when we slit the paper towel tube from top to bottom and flatten it out? Or what happens if I use a scalpel to slit the skin on my chest from my navel to my neck? In both cases we have concrete examples of how the lateral surface area of all right circular cylinders is the area of a rectangle whose width is the height of the original cylinder and whose length is the circumference of the original cylinder. That's why the surface area is $2\pi r$ (the circumference) times h (height) plus the two circles on the top and bottom ($2\pi r^2$).

Despite all this excitement and good thinking, we still don't really know how much each of our students has taken away from this lesson. That's why it's time to hand out the homework that enables students to solidify as well as extend their understandings.

> **Homework:** Doctors estimate the amount of skin each person has using the formula
> $$S = 0.6h^2$$
> where S is the number of square inches of skin and h is the person's height in inches.
>
> Use the formula to determine a reasonable estimate for how much skin you have. Then validate your result using a referent such as an $8\frac{1}{2} \times 11$ sheet of paper *and* using surface area formulas. Discuss the reasons for the differences among your three estimates.

At a much simpler level, consider placing the following information on the board or passing it out on a sheet of paper

Carmelo's Pizza	
Small Pies	**Medium Pies**
6 inches in diameter	9 inches in diameter
6 slices	8 slices
$5.75	$8.95

My favorite approach is merely to present the data, as we saw in Chapter 7, and ask a class to work in groups of two or three to answer the question "So?" So, what might we care about if we have to decide what to buy? It doesn't take long to generate much more than one class worth of interesting mathematics to deal with such questions as:

- Which pizza is the better buy?

- How much cheaper is one slice of the small pizza?

- How much bigger or smaller is one slice of the medium pizza than one slice of the small pizza?

- I need to feed 20 people, and each person should get about 25 square inches of pizza. Which pizzas should I buy, how many, and what will it cost?

- What percent more is the diameter of the medium pizza relative to the diameter of the small pizza? What percent larger is the area of the medium pizza relative to the area of the small pizza?

- Design and describe a large pizza, including its diameter, the number of slices, and its cost. Explain how you made your choices.

Imagine, in similar fashion, what ensues when we launch a lesson with questions like:

- How big is your desk?
- How many sheets of paper are needed to cover the bulletin board?
- How many rolls of toilet paper would it take to surround the school?
- What's the average weight of our loaded backpacks as we leave to go home?
- About how heavy is our heaviest textbook?
- Could a pen draw a line a mile long?
- Could we fit the entire student body of the school into our classroom?
- Could 5000 people fit into the school's cafeteria?

Thus, when we are searching for interesting and thought-provoking contexts from which to build effective mathematics lessons, and when we are seeking fodder for the language, review, picture-drawing, and number sense strategies we've discussed, there is rarely a better place to turn than the worlds of data and measurement.

SO WHAT SHOULD WE SEE IN AN EFFECTIVE MATHEMATICS CLASSROOM?

- Lots of questions are included that ask: How big? How far? How much? How many?
- Measurement is an ongoing part of daily instruction and the entry point for a much larger chunk of the curriculum.
- Students are frequently asked to find and estimate measures, to use measuring, and to describe the relative size of measures that arise during instruction.
- The teacher offers frequent reminders that much measurement is referential—that is, we use a referent (such as your height or a sheet of paper) to estimate measures.

Just Don't Do It!

9

INSTRUCTIONAL SHIFT 8

Minimize what is no longer important, and teach what is important when it is appropriate to do so.

I believe, as this book suggests, that we will get the greatest impact on student achievement by making a set of strategic shifts in instructional practice. But although changing *how* we deliver instruction is likely to account for the lion's share of improvement, there is also the pesky issue of changing some of *what* we teach and *when* we teach it. There are topics that it just does not make sense to continue to teach. There are topics that should be postponed by a year to give all students a realistic chance at mastery. And there are textbooks stuffed with extra material that no one can possibly cover and that wise teachers strategically omit.

Try this: What is the formula for the volume of a sphere? Really, do you know it? Have you forgotten it? Do you ever use it? Do you even care? When I ask teachers for this piece of mathematical trivia, I am typically greeted by nervous laughs. A few (those who have recently taught the topic) proudly call out the answer, and a few (those with a very warped view of mathematics) appear completely mortified that they don't know or don't remember it. But the vast majority wisely don't really care that they can't provide an immediate and correct answer and know that there are many places to find the formula if and when it is needed.

But now return to our middle school and high school classes where memorizing and regurgitating the formula $V = \frac{4}{3}\pi r^3$ is a perfect way to sort students out on the basis of memorization criteria that have little relation to understanding volume and actually using the formula. This is despite the fact that on *every* SAT, ACT, GRE, and high-stakes state test, there is a formula sheet with the formula for the volume of a sphere provided to all test takers. Consider this disconnect between, on the one hand, classroom expectations for memorizing a formula for which few normal human beings maintain immediate recallable knowledge and, on the other hand, relevant real-world needs for understanding how much $\frac{4}{3}$ is, what π is equal to, what the r represents, and what that little elevated 3 means—that is, how to *use* the formula once it is presented. Consider the difference between a focus on the elements of the formula and where the formula comes from, and typical expectations for simply memorizing a string of symbols and plugging numbers in for r.

This simple exercise demonstrates that there are times and places where our curricular expectations—in this case the mindless memorization of complex formulas—are out of step with real-world needs and expectations. It opens the door to important questions about what, in the early years of the twenty-first century, is still essential "baby" to the mathematics curriculum and requires ever greater emphasis, and what is increasingly "bath water" that should be tossed away to make precious time for the "baby."

Clearly, these are nuanced and often controversial decisions. Of course basic number facts are part of the essential "baby" of learning mathematics, and pencil-and-paper algorithms for multiplying and dividing by 1-digit factors or divisors still have an important place in the curriculum. But what about computing with 2- and 3-digit factors and divisors? How much time is devoted to these increasingly obsolete skills and how many students stumble trying to jump these computational hurdles? And couldn't this time be put to much better use?

So what mathematical content is increasingly "bath water" that wastes valuable time and does little to support mathematics success for all students? The standard I use is "Do I really care whether my children and grandchildren know and can do this?" That is, if I am not convinced that my own children will be disadvantaged by *not* learning something, why would I impose that content on someone else's children? Here is what emerges when I apply this standard:

- Multi-digit multiplication and division. When was the last time you used pencil and paper to find the quotient of 2953 and 15.9?

- Sevenths and ninths. When was the last time you encountered a seventh or a ninth in everyday life? Because nearly all encounters with fractions are limited to ruler fractions such as $\frac{1}{2}$, $\frac{1}{4}$, $\frac{1}{8}$, and $\frac{1}{16}$, thirds and sixths, and fifths and tenths, one has to question the need to find a common denominator for fifths and elevenths. Only in a textbook in a math class do we impose the lunacy of $\frac{3}{13} + \frac{4}{7}$!

- Complex, rarely used formulas. Here we can take our cue from the formula sheets provided with the tests that students face to help us decide what formulas all students need to know *without* reference to a formula sheet—for example, the formulas for the areas of rectangles and triangles. But memorizing many of the surface area and volume formulas for spheres, cylinders, pyramids, and cones is no longer worth the time or effort.

- Simplifying radicals. We really have to pause and consider why anyone would believe that $\frac{1}{\sqrt{2}}$ is *not* an acceptable answer but somehow its "simplified" equivalent $\frac{\sqrt{2}}{2}$ is! In a world of calculators and decimal equivalents, spending time "simplifying" $\frac{6}{\sqrt{10} - \sqrt{7}}$ by multiplying both numerator and denominator by the conjugate $\sqrt{10} + \sqrt{7}$ to get the "simplified" expression $2(\sqrt{10} + \sqrt{7})$ just doesn't make sense. What *is* important when students encounter an expression like $\frac{6}{\sqrt{10} - \sqrt{7}}$ is the number sense to see that $\sqrt{10}$ is a little more than 3 and that $\sqrt{7}$ is about $2\frac{1}{2}$, so the value of the expression is about $6 \div \frac{1}{2}$, or about 12. Interestingly enough, the approximate decimal equivalent to this expression is 11.62, so 12 isn't a bad estimate at all.

- Factoring. When we consider all of the possible quadratic trinomials in the formula $ax^2 + bx + c$, where a, b, and c are all non-zero integers between -10 and 10, we discover that there are $20 \times 20 \times 20$, or 8000, possible trinomials, of which only about 250, or 3%, can be factored into binomials with integral roots. It's pretty amazing—some would say foolish—that we spend so much time on a skill that has such limited value once we leave the neat confines of contrived problems and orderly exercises.

Accessible Mathematics

The question of what content is no longer essential is closely related to the issue of when specific content should be taught and what content is best postponed for a year. My thinking is that higher standards should not mean teaching more math and harder math to more students at earlier and earlier grades. Unfortunately, too often this is exactly what teachers face. With the best of intentions, ignorant or intimidated policy makers, often with the support of upper-middle-class parents, who continue to see schools as sorting machines designed to protect the interests of their children, sign off on the mastery of multi-digit long division by all students by the end of grade 5 or the mastery of subtraction with regrouping by second grade or, more recently, the mindless mandate for traditional Algebra I for all eighth graders, without due consideration to either the wide-ranging implications of these edicts or what it would take to come close to achieving them.

The result of these topic placement and curriculum mandates is that all too often, teachers and their students are set up to fail. We ignore everything we know about normal distributions and the diversity of learners when we take a skill that can be mastered by *some* students by, say, fourth grade and mandate its mastery by *all* students by the end of fourth grade. Subtraction with regrouping is a perfect example. When I went to school, back in the so-called good old days, when math supposedly worked for most people, this important skill was expected at the end of third grade. That way, teachers and students had sufficient time to develop the stronger sense of place value required to understand regrouping (or borrowing, as we called it then), as well as time to strengthen student mastery of addition and subtraction facts.

So why has this skill crept down to second grade where it gives most teachers and most students so much trouble? Simple. One or two subtraction with regrouping items were appropriately placed on norm-referenced standardized tests given to second graders for the sole purpose of discriminating between those students in the 90th percentile and those in the 95th percentile. How else could these distinctions be made unless we put items on the test that most students were *not* expected to get correct? But as testing and accountability became more and more important, school administrators looked more and more carefully at the tests. If the second-grade test asked students to subtract with regrouping, well then, appropriate or not, we'd better teach it to all our second graders. From there such skills got codified in state and local curriculum guides and then added to traditional textbooks, where subtraction with regrouping now appears in second grade, in third grade, and again in fourth grade.

It is easy to describe a similar inappropriate and downward progression for addition and subtraction of fractions in fourth grade, well before most students even have a sense of the meaning of a fraction, or for computing with percents, which was rarely taught before seventh grade two decades ago but is now a standard and very problematic practice in sixth grade.

And what happens when we try to ram such skills down the throats of students prematurely? Students get frustrated and give up on mathematics and themselves, convinced they're not smart enough to learn it. Teachers get frustrated with mandates that are impossible to achieve but forge onward, knowing that it will work for some of their students. The bottom line, as affirmed by all of the recent international studies, is that our students pay a serious price for the fundamentally fragmented and incoherent mathematics curriculum that is the U.S. norm.

Alternatively, my thinking is that higher standards ought to mean a non-negotiable expectation that all students (not just 30% or 60%) master a set of reasonable mathematical skills. For example, the following 1-year postponements might restore sanity to the curricular program and represent realistic expectations:

- expecting nearly all students to demonstrate mastery of subtraction with and without regrouping by the end of third grade instead of second grade

- expecting nearly all students to demonstrate quick recall of all addition and subtraction facts by the end of third grade instead of second grade

- expecting nearly all students to demonstrate quick recall of all multiplication and division facts by the end of fifth grade instead of fourth grade

- expecting nearly all students to demonstrate mastery of addition and subtraction of reasonable fractions by the end of fifth grade instead of fourth grade.

Accessible Mathematics

Sure, some students can master these skills at the earlier grade, but there is no way to raise mathematics achievement by ignoring what classroom teachers have known for years: many students need more time or aren't ready, no matter how powerful the instruction. A sane approach would be to err on the side of more students later and fewer students earlier. Unfortunately, this is not the prescribed reality that exists in most states and districts, but it could easily be the adopted reality in most schools and classrooms.

Finally, there is the pressure to "finish the book," in spite of the impossibility of effectively "covering" the content in a book of more than 800 pages. But remember that every publisher, striving to meet the widely disparate demands of fifty different state curriculum guidelines, must stuff far more material into every textbook than anyone could possibly cover in a year. One approach is simply to skip the last two chapters in any textbook, confident that doing so will only help your students. You won't rush through the important content, and you'll be skipping the material that probably shouldn't be taught at that grade in the first place.

SO WHAT SHOULD WE SEE IN AN EFFECTIVE MATHEMATICS CLASSROOM?

- A curriculum of skills, concepts, and applications that are reasonable to expect all students to master, and not those skills, concepts, and applications that have gradually been moved to an earlier grade on the basis of inappropriately raising standards
- Implementation of a district and state curriculum that includes essential skills and understandings for a world of calculators and computers, and not what many recognize as too much content to cover at each grade level
- A deliberate questioning of the appropriateness of the mathematical content, regardless of what may or may not be on the high-stakes state test, in every grade and course

Putting It All in Context

10

INSTRUCTIONAL SHIFT 9

Embed the mathematics in realistic problems and real-world contexts.

Try to envision what it's like to be a student in fourth-period math in most any middle school or high school in America. Chances are, on the board, you are greeted by an objective of the day ("Use rates and unit rates") and a predetermined, practice-rich homework assignment encoded into strange fractions like:

$$\frac{229}{1 - 19\text{odd}} \quad \frac{224}{2 - 22\text{even}} \quad \frac{219}{31,34,36}.$$

As we have seen, after an essentially useless review of the previous night's homework, you get to observe and listen to the process of solving two examples that few normal human beings are likely to care about. This show and tell is prelude to the opportunity to work individually on several similar problems under that rubric of "guided practice." Not exactly a process or an environment particularly conducive to high levels of engagement or learning but, on the basis of extensive research and my own personal experience, the overwhelming norm.

Envision instead walking into exactly the same classroom and, immediately following 6 minutes of mini-math review, your teacher opens a colorful copy of the *Guinness Book of World Records* and uses a computer or overhead projector to post the following statement: "Peter Dowdeswell of London, England, holds the world record for pancake consumption." Once again, context—in this case an intriguing food consumption record—is a powerful motivator of students and attractor of interest and attention. So let's observe how this might play out.

TEACHER: Is there anything you would like to know?

MICHELLE: Yes, how many pancakes he ate.

TEACHER: And why is that?

MICHELLE: Because it's a world record and I want to know the number of pancakes he ate.

RODNEY: I want to know how big they were. If he ate a lot of very small pancakes, it's not as impressive as if he ate a lot of normal or big pancakes.

TEACHER: So, what information would help you with the size of the pancakes, Rodney?

RODNEY: I guess I'd like to know the diameter of each pancake, assuming they are round.

TEACHER: Anything else?

LATICIA: I think we'd need to know the thickness too, so we'd have a sense of the volume of each pancake. But I also think we'd need to know how long.

TEACHER: You mean "how long" like 20 inches?

LATICIA: No. I mean like 2 minutes or 2 hours.

CATE: Don't we also need to know how big the guy is and whether there was butter and syrup?

TEACHER: Wonderful. Here is what the *Guinness Book of World Records* says: "He consumed 62 pancakes each 6 inches in diameter and $\frac{3}{8}$ inches thick, with butter and syrup, in 6 minutes and 58.5 seconds."

After writing or displaying the relevant data on the board, the teacher asks, "So what would be interesting or informative about this?" Working in pairs or triplets and spending a few minutes formulating their answers, students, already motivated by the context, are likely to pose a rich array of questions that are easily translated into problems for you to use, assign, add to, amend, or simply save for a test:

• About how high a stack would that be? (requiring students to estimate $\frac{3}{8} \times 62$)

- Exactly how high a stack would that be? (requiring students to calculate $\frac{3}{8} \times 62$)

- At what rate did he consume the pancakes? (requiring students to identify the 62 pancakes and the 7 minutes, in order to estimate 9 pancakes per minute or about 0.15 pancakes per second)

- How much pancake must he have eaten each second? (requiring students to construct about $\frac{1}{7}$ of a pancake 6 inches in diameter, or about one mouthful)

- How much pancake did he actually consume? (requiring students to calculate the volume of the stack)

- Can you show about how big that is? (requiring students to describe or visualize about 650 cubic inches)

- How is it possible that someone with a stomach that our biology book says is only about 150 cubic inches could possibly eat that much pancake? (which opens the door to some very interesting conjectures about whether the pancake stays down or in and what's left of the dough after all the air comes out)

- Can you graph his progress? (requiring students to conjure up the shape of the line or curve that connects the point (0, 0) on a coordinate grid to the point (7, 62) representing the 62 pancakes consumed in just under 7 minutes and to connect the reality of slowing down to a curve on the grid)

- How big would a single pancake $\frac{3}{8}$ inch thick have to be if it has the same volume? (requiring students to set two formulas equal and solve for the radius)

In an earlier grade it might be a restaurant menu or price list; in another grade it might be grocery store register tapes or, as we'll see, drug testing. But in all cases, we can choose either to walk the straight and narrow and present the mathematics devoid of any reason for many students to care *or* to embed the mathematics we need to teach in contexts that are much more likely to engage our students and forestall the "When are we ever gonna use this?" question.

So let's take a closer look at what we are choosing between. On the one hand we have the straight and narrow, albeit familiar and comfortable, mathematics of "Find the quotient: $15 \div 2.29$."

Accessible Mathematics

It is not hard to imagine the "teaching" that now ensues. We might briefly spice things up by asking what types of numbers are in the "problem" or what operation is required. But sooner or later we get down to the procedures. Most teachers can hear themselves asking, "Is there a decimal point on the outside, boys and girls?" Upon getting the obvious answer that there is one, we turn to "And what do you think we do with the decimal point on the outside? That's right. We move it! Exactly. And which way do you think we should move it, boys and girls? Great. To the right! And how many places do I have to move it? Fine. Two places to the right."

It's not surprising that the only question not likely to be asked is "Why?" But why would we ask "Why?" when no one really knows, or when the real answer is that "it's the rule," or when we don't want to take the time to explain that moving the decimal point two places to the right is the same as multiplying by 100 and when we multiply both the divisor and the dividend by 100, the quotient doesn't change. Like I said, why ask "Why?" when the goal is getting students to memorize and practice the steps in a procedure that nearly all normal people have replaced with a simple calculator?

But back to that stirring division problem: "Now that we've moved the decimal point on the outside two places, what do you think we do with the other one?" Even first-year teachers recognize the stupidity of this question as it comes out of their mouths. Why are we moving decimal points around in the first place? Besides, when the dividend is a whole number, most students think there isn't a decimal point "on the inside" in the first place. But finally, we tell our students to "move the other decimal point two places to the right as well, move it up (for another unexplained reason), and divide the way we've always divided."

I sit in the back of the room muttering, "Try an estimate! Explain why! Give them a reason to care!" as I watch a roomful of eyes glaze over. It is so clear why mathematics fails to work for so many students.

But there is a clear alternative. Ask yourself: When do normal human beings do the mathematics I am teaching? What situations arise in daily life where people use this mathematics? In this case, one of many answers is deciding how many of something you can afford to buy. So let's return to the same class with the same objective and listen in as the teacher announces that everyone has $15 and we have Burger King Whopper coupons that lower the cost of Whoppers with Cheese to $2.29. Instead of "What's the quotient?" or immediately asking "How many can I afford to buy?" the question is "So?" and here is what I've seen emerge:

- What's the change if you only buy one?
- How many can you buy?
- What about sales tax?
- About how many can you get?
- Can you get 10 Whoppers?
- Suppose I want fries and a soda. How many friends can I take to Burger King?

Look at how some of this plays out. When you follow up on "Can you get 10 Whoppers?" there is usually a very quick negative response. It gets interesting when you follow up with "How do you know?" Some students explain that "10 would be $22.90," while others explain that "They're more than $1.50." Here is reasoning and justification at its best in a class where *all* students get to see and hear that "10 Whoppers would be $22.90 because you move the decimal point, but you only have $15" on the one hand *and* "If they were $1.50 each, you could buy 10, but they're more than that, so you can't get 10" on the other. Who would ever have thought that a simple "Can you get 10?" would open the conceptual doors to inverse relationships. That is, for a given amount of money, the higher the price, the fewer you can buy, or, more technically, for a given dividend, the greater the divisor, the smaller the quotient, and the smaller the divisor, the greater the quotient. We know how important this concept is, and we know how hard it is to explain in the abstract. It begins to take root when we have only $15 for Whoppers or a $100 gift certificate to spend on CDs.

Then there is the issue of estimation. A reasonable estimate in this case is 5 or 6 or 7, but in all cases, any estimate is only as good as its justification. So here are some of the answers we would look for:

- "About 5 because 2.29 rounds up to $3, and 15 divided by 3 is 5—plus there's probably tax."
- "About 6 because $2.50 and $2.50 is $5, so 4 for $10 and about 6 for $15."
- "About 7 because $2.29 is a little more than 2, and 15 divided by 2 is about 7."

Accessible Mathematics

The question isn't which is the best estimate, but whether we have a reasonable estimate so that when we take out our calculators and divide 15 by 2.29 (getting 6.5502183), we know that we're in the ballpark and that we can buy exactly 6 Whoopers without tax, and in this case, unless the tax is in the range of 10%, we can buy exactly 6 *including* tax as well.

Next there is the issue of how the calculators open doors to understanding operations and negative numbers. The fact that some students relate the question "How many can we afford?" to division doesn't mean that all students will, or even should, make this connection. I've watched students very successfully enter 2.29 + 2.29 and then repeat the = key as they count to 6 and get 13.74. They hit = one more time, and the calculator shows 16.03 or too much. These students have used repetitive addition to "buy" Whoppers and have figured out that they can afford only 6. Another student just as successfully enters 15 and successively subtracts 2.29 to get 12.71, 10.42, 8.13, 5.84, 3.55 and 1.26, discovering that he'll have $1.26 left after buying 6, which isn't enough for another one. Still another student follows this same procedure and hits the = key one more time, resulting in −1.03, which can be interpreted as how much the student needs to borrow from his mom to get a seventh Whopper. And in the end, the teacher-led discussion relates division to repetitive subtraction and shows how the four basic operations are interrelated.

Several obvious questions arise from this comparison of approaches: Which class do you want your own child to be in? Which class do you want your nephews and nieces and brothers and sisters to be in? Which class do the young people of this country deserve? Which class will help us meet the important goals of much broader mathematical literacy and much higher levels of student achievement?

You can choose the class that basically communicates "Shut up and follow the rules of moving decimal points to get an answer no one cares about" and then immediately progresses to a 20-problem drill and practice worksheet. Or you can choose the $15 and $2.29 Whoppers class that incorporates a real-world context, estimation, number sense, and alternative approaches and ends with the formative assessment check when the teacher asks, "How many Whoppers can you afford if you have found another $5 and now have $20 and the price is reduced to $1.89 each in a city with a 6% sales tax?"

But once again, the critical question is "Why bother?" Teaching this way is harder to do. This type of instruction takes longer to plan, it is often very messy as we share instructional power with our students, and its success can be harder to measure. A brief history provides a clearer perspective on exactly why it's worth doing.

In 1989, President George H. W. Bush and Bill Clinton (then governor of Arkansas and the chair of the National Governors Association) joined forces to deliver a set of national education goals. One of the goals—and the one deemed by many to be most unattainable—was that the United States would be first in the world in mathematics and science by 2000. Such an ambitious goal had worked in the 1960s when President Kennedy called for the United States to land a man on the moon by the end of the decade. In the case of a man on the moon, there was ample funding, a broad scientific mobilization, and a national infrastructure coordinated by NASA to get the job done. In the case of math and science, there was no national mobilization, no real new funding, and no analysis of why we were so far from number 1. Instead, Goals 2000 was limited to top-down exhortation to 50 states and 15,000 school districts. It took until about 1994 before it became clear this goal would never be met, and the entire National Educational Goals Panel fell to the wayside.

But that didn't stop the top-down policy makers and their penchant for exhortation and unattainable goals. If we weren't going to be number 1 in the world, then at least all students should take Algebra I, given its importance as a gateway to high school success. After all, math is such an easy target with its straightforward skills and its identifiable courses. So state after state moved to mandate Algebra I without changing the curriculum, without improving instruction practices or assessments, and without adequate funding for the professional development that is needed if Algebra I truly is to work for all students. No sooner was the "Algebra for All" bandwagon well under way than California, hijacked by a tight cadre of research mathematicians, decided that everyone should do Algebra I in eighth grade! We hadn't yet figured out how to make Algebra I successful for ninth graders, and already the pressure was on to make it work for all eighth graders.

This process of setting impossible goals that are predicated on wishing for improvement without acknowledging the curricular and instructional changes that must accompany any such improvement has continued unabated. In 2002 *No Child Left Behind* told us that every student must be proficient in mathematics by 2014. Once again, an admirable goal, but by 2007 it became clear that such a goal was statistically impossible—and that even to come close would require far more funding and institutional change than the system seemed willing or able to make.

The latest such mathematical boondoggle, conveniently ignoring the failure of each of these previous goals, is the audacity of mandating Algebra II for every student as the essential indicator of the integrity of the high school diploma. This goal is based on correlational (not cause-and-effect) data showing that those students who successfully complete Algebra II in high school are much more likely to go to college and to succeed in college than those students who don't take or aren't successful in Algebra II. If ever there was a case for adding statistical thinking to the mathematics curriculum, it's right here. What a surprise that when the brightest or most school-adaptable students pass Algebra II, they are more likely to be successful after high school! But is the variable the taking of and the content of Algebra II, or is it the pool of students who happen to succeed in Algebra II? That question has not been answered.

My problem, and the source of my frustration, is that I support these ambitious goals. Like so many other dedicated educators, I am committed to finding ways to ensure that mathematical achievement increases significantly. But we don't need more study or more data to know that the secret to raising mathematics achievement is high-quality instruction in important and relevant mathematical content. We don't need more study to tell us that, just as we have never managed to teach all students how to divide by 2- and 3-digit numbers with pencil and paper, we are not going to be able to take the traditional 1960s algebra curriculum and successfully ram it down the throats of the Nintendo generation. Instead of codifying the narrow set of symbol manipulation skills that constitute the heart of Algebra I and Algebra II, we should be focusing on algebraic thinking, on the application of functions in the real world, on modeling, and on statistics. Instead of continuing to mandate a curriculum that has always served to sort kids out, we need a curriculum that truly engages and empowers and that is taught in ways that research affirms make a real difference. We need a curriculum that is assessed by a set of assessments that should be passed by every legislator who votes for the tests and every teacher who teaches the students who will take the tests. We need a curriculum and accompanying instruction that make mathematics accessible to students.

So how do we make algebra accessible to far more students? How do we begin to achieve the goals of algebra for all? Once again, we can choose. In Algebra I we can continue to limit instruction to the likes of

Given: $F = 4 (S - 65) + 10$

Find F when $S = 81$

Or we can inform our class that: The speeding fine in Vermont is $4 for every mile per hour over the 65 mph limit, plus a $10 handling fee. Then we can build algebraic understanding from questions such as:

- What is the fine if you are caught going 81 miles per hour?
- How fast must you have been going if the fine was $102?
- Create a graph that shows the relationship between the speed and the fine.

And in Algebra II we can continue to teach nineteenth-century math to twenty-first-century students by asking our students to

Solve for x: $16 (.75)^x < 1$

Or we can inform our class that: You ingest 16 mg of a controlled substance at 8 a.m. If your body metabolizes 25% of the substance each hour, could you pass a drug test at 4 p.m. if the legal limit is 1 mg?

It should be clear that in each case, the former approach continues what we've always done and what clearly has had only limited success and has not served the broader needs of all students. The latter approach acknowledges that many students need different modes of access to mathematical concepts to be successful. It should be clear that we will never attain the important and ambitious goals of algebra for all specifically, and mathematical power for all generally, until and unless we change how the material is taught.

SO WHAT SHOULD WE SEE IN AN EFFECTIVE MATHEMATICS CLASSROOM?

- Frequent embedding of the mathematical skills and concepts in real-world situations and contexts
- Frequent use of "So, what questions arise from these data or this situation?"
- Problems that emerge from teachers asking, "When and where do normal human beings encounter the mathematics I need to teach?"

Just Ask Them "Why?"

11

INSTRUCTIONAL SHIFT 10

Make "Why?" "How do you know?" and "Can you explain?"
classroom mantras.

Last and most powerfully, just ask them "Why?" Failing to follow up a student's answer with "Why?" or "How did you get that answer?" or "Can you explain your thinking?" is another serious missed opportunity I observe in classroom after classroom. It's as though we're programmed to receive the "right answer." Once it is received, often from as few as a handful of students, we assume that all is well and that it must be time to move on to the next question. More specifically, here's the classroom dynamic I often hear: "Aida, what kind of triangle is this?" Aida correctly responds "isosceles." The teacher, smiling or nodding, responds "good" and moves immediately to "And Max, what kind of triangle is this?" I'm left silently screaming, in utter exasperation, "But *why* is it isosceles, Aida?"

Or think about any of the hundreds of two- or three-word or one-number answers that pass for discourse in the typical mathematics class: "A proportion," "Eighty-five," "The square root of three," or "They're congruent." Fine, but what we also want to know—in fact, what we need to know—in all classrooms is "Why do we need a proportion?" "How did you get eighty-five?" "Why isn't it the square root of five?" and "Can you explain why they're congruent?"

Consider what emerges from the simple scenario of asking Aida "Why?" Not uncommonly, she will respond with something like "Because it has two equal sides," which now serves as the perfect launching pad for the teacher to ask, "Anyone else?" This in turn is likely to elicit statements such as "Because it has two congruent sides" and "Because it has two sides of equal length" and "Because the base angles are congruent." Such discourse reinforces your commitment to a language-rich classroom. It opens the door to a classroom culture of justifying all answers and to an atmosphere that respects and encourages alternative answers.

When we reflect on our classroom dynamics or observe our lessons on videotape, we see that rarely are more than half the hands raised when we ask a question and that rarely does more than a quarter of the class regularly call out answers. That leaves a lot of room in every class for students who don't know the answer, aren't certain of the answer, are wary of volunteering what might be a wrong answer, or simply don't care. Creating an environment where *all* students in the class get to hear explanations or justifications and where multiple explanations are valued makes it far safer for students to take intellectual risks. Beyond providing critical insight into students' thinking and understanding, these classroom dynamics often result in unexpected, yet still correct, answers.

For anyone unsure of the power of just asking "Why?" or unaware of how rarely it is employed in many classes, consider what happens when you dare to question the correct answer proposed by one of the brightest students in your class with something as simple and innocuous as "Really?" The student's typically flustered response "What did I do wrong?" suggests that he or she is only questioned for wrong answers and is almost never asked to explain correct answers.

But perhaps most damaging is how incorrect answers are commonly responded to. I hear teachers responding, often with the best of intentions to provide appropriate feedback, "No," "Wrong," "Not quite," "Come on, James, think," or any number of variations of what I suspect, based on body language, is interpreted by the student as simply "You're dumb." And then we wonder why we have such a serious motivation problem with so many students!

Accordingly, any time a student provides a correct answer, when the answer is greeted with "Why?" or its equivalent:

- You might hear a sound explanation that informs both you and the other students in the class.
- You might hear a flawed explanation that reveals the thinness of the student's understanding or the student's inability to put his or her thinking into words.

- You have the opportunity to ask other students to provide alternative explanations.
- You have the opportunity to ask other students to put an explanation they have heard into their own words.

And any time a student provides an incorrect answer, when that answer too is greeted with "Why?" or its equivalent:

- The student might recognize his or her error and self-correct in public, thereby sending the message that justifications are just as valued as correct answers.
- The student reveals the error or misconception that led to the incorrect answer, a misconception that is likely to be shared by others in the class.
- You sidestep the need to say "No" or "Wrong."
- You can momentarily let the error pass and turn to other students for their thinking before returning to the original student.

In all of these cases, consistently following up most answers with a request for an explanation conveys the powerful message that good mathematical thinking *begins* with an answer. It supports a thinking curriculum that values justification and serves as a foundation for building a language-rich classroom. Moreover, implementing this strategy conveys the expectation that students can learn from each other as well as from their teachers and thereby helps to build an effective classroom community of learners. All this because of the simple, consistent use of "Why?"

SO WHAT SHOULD WE SEE IN AN EFFECTIVE MATHEMATICS CLASSROOM?

- Every student answer is responded to with a request for justification.
- Both teachers and students consistently and frequently use "Why?" "Can you explain that?" "How do you know?" or equivalent questions.
- Dismissive responses such as "No," "Wrong," "Not quite," and their equivalents are absent from the classroom.

Punting Is Simply No Longer Acceptable

12

Implementing the shifts that we have discussed is *hard*, it takes *time*, and it takes deliberate *planning*. It is not uncommon to ask to see a lesson plan and get something close to the following penciled into a $2 \times 2\frac{1}{2}$-inch box in a plan book:

SOLVING PROPORTIONS

Do pg. 343 Examples 1 and 3 on the board
Guided practice p. 345 2, 4, and 10

HW: $\dfrac{346}{11\text{–}25 \text{ odd}}$ $\dfrac{342}{8\text{–}20 \text{ even}}$ $\dfrac{335}{1, 34, 39}$

This plan tells us

- the topic to be addressed in the broadest of terms
- the two examples, drawn from the textbook, that will be used to show how to solve proportions

- the individual practice and homework exercises that will be assigned.

However, this plan does not tell us

- whether the examples will include a discussion of what a proportion is, why proportions are so important, when they are used, and why cross-multiplying and dividing is one technique for solving proportions
- whether the unit rate method to solving proportions will be addressed
- whether the need for proportions will be grounded in real-world contexts
- how a proportion is a multiplicative, as opposed to an additive, relationship
- what common errors or misconceptions can be expected and how they will be addressed
- how students will be expected to participate in the lesson, individually as well as collaboratively
- exactly how student understanding will be monitored and assessed.

Back when math wasn't expected to work for all students, and back when we worked under far fewer demands for accountability, this type of planning may have worked. After all, this was pretty much the way we were taught and the way we were taught to teach. Before there were calculators and computers, and before we understood the central role of problem solving and the application of mathematical understandings, this type of minimalist planning may have sufficed. But today's realities are vastly different. We *are* expected to find ways to make math work for far more kids. We *do* live in a world of calculators and computers and in a world that expects, even requires, deeper understanding and far greater problem-solving skill. That's why our lessons must be more carefully planned. That's why bare-bones lesson plans of objectives, examples, exercises, and homework need to be broadened and why last-minute "punting" needs to be banished. And that's why effective planning of lessons must address all of those elements that the typical minimalist plan doesn't.

I've observed too many classes where the absence of planning was all too evident. It was obvious that the teacher had not worked out the assigned problems ahead of time to determine the nuances that emerge from them. It was apparent that little thought had been given to the conceptual hurdles that are most likely to arise and how to address them both before and after they emerge. It was clear that the primary objective was "teaching" students how to memorize and correctly use a procedure to get right answers, with very little attention to understanding why the procedure works or where the procedure is applied.

But the answer *isn't* the unwieldy four-page lesson plan forms that I've seen used for lesson study seminars. It is simply neither reasonable nor a productive use of time to complete three or four page forms for every lesson one teaches. Nor is the answer top-down mandates for more and better planning when teachers are provided no additional time to get it done. Rather, the answer is a professionally reasonable set of expectations that, for every lesson, careful consideration be given, prior to teaching the lesson, to the following:

- The mathematical content of the lesson. That is, what skills or concepts are being developed or mastered as a result of the lesson? Often, teachers who plan effective lessons back-map the content from asking, "Exactly what do I expect my students to know or be able to do at the end of this lesson?"

- The mathematical tasks of the lesson. That is, what specific questions, problems, tasks, investigations, or activities will students be working on during the lesson? Often, this includes the worksheets that are prepared for the lesson and identifies the references or materials that are needed.

- Evidence that the lesson was successful. That is, deliberate consideration of what performances will convince you (and any outside observer) that most, if not all, of your students have accomplished your objective.

- Launch and closure. That is, pausing after delineating the above, planning exactly how you will use the first 5 minutes of the lesson, and outlining exactly what summary will close the lesson and pro-vide a foreshadowing of tomorrow.

- Notes and nuances. That is, a set of reminders about vocabulary, connections, common mistakes, and typical misconceptions that need to be considered *before* the lesson and kept in mind during it.

- Resources and homework. That is, what materials or resources are essential for students to successfully complete the lesson tasks or activities? And exactly what follow-up homework tasks, problems, and/or exercises will be assigned upon the completion of the lesson?

- Post-lesson reflections. That is, a home for the inevitable "If only …" realizations that should be noted to inform your planning the next time.

Rather than three- or four-page tomes, effective lessons can be effectively planned on a single page that outlines these seven areas of consideration. See Figure 12-1 for a model lesson-planning template.

Figure 12-2 shows a completed lesson plan as a model for the information and level of detail that reflect deliberate, yet reasonable, planning.

Figure 12-1   Lesson Planning Template

Lesson Objective or Purpose: What mathematical skills and understanding will be developed?

—

—

—

Lesson Tasks, Problems, and Activities (attach worksheets):

—

—

—

—

Evidence of Success: What exactly do I expect students to be able to do at the end of the lesson, and how will I know?

Lesson Launch Notes:	Lesson Closure Notes:

Notes and Nuances: Vocabulary, connections, common mistakes, typical misconceptions, etc.

Resources:	Homework:

Post-Lesson Reflections:

Figure 12-2   Model Lesson Plan

Lesson Objective or Purpose: What mathematical skills and understandings will be developed?

— Correctly depicting successive stages of a growing tile pattern
— Using words to describe a growing tile pattern
— Completing a table for the first several stages of a growing tile pattern
— Finding and justifying a rule for any stage of a growing tile pattern

Lesson Tasks, Problems, and Activities (attach worksheets)

1. Launch—see below
2. Distribute worksheet and ask students to work in pairs to complete the five questions.
3. Have pairs of students share their patterns, tables, rules, and justifications with the class.
4. Lead large-group discussion and demonstration of the constant and variable parts of the pattern and of the equivalence of all correct versions of the rules.
5. Assign homework and wrap up by reiterating points in closure notes.

Evidence of Success: What exactly do I expect students to be able to do at the end of the lesson, and how will I know?

My students will correctly depict stages 4 and 5 of the pattern, build a table that shows evidence of constant and variable parts, and find a correct rule for any stage of the pattern. They will be able to explain their reasoning and justify their conclusions.

Lesson Launch Notes	**Lesson Closure Notes**
— Set context—explore and mathematize a predictable growing pattern. — Look at an H pattern as preparation for each of you creating and mathematizing a growing tile pattern based on one of your own initials.	— Look at how different interpretations of the pattern result in different expressions. — Emphasize that all mathematically correct rules are valued and can be shown to be equivalent.

Notes and Nuances: Vocabulary, connections, common mistakes, typical misconceptions, etc.

— Constant vs. variable part of the pattern and where these parts appear in the drawings, the table, and the rule
— Iterative (add five each time) vs. explicit ($5 N + 2$) rules and the limitations of the iterative
— Help students see that there is more than one correct form for the rule and that all correct rules are equivalent

Resources: 1. *Lessons for Algebraic Thinking, Grades 6–8*, Lawrence and Hennessy, Math Solutions Publications; 2. *Fostering Algebraic Thinking*, Driscoll and Heinemann	**Homework:** Provide students with another pattern of square tiles (for example, a growing L-shape pattern) and ask them to find a rule and use it to determine how many tiles are needed for stage 100 of the pattern.

Post-Lesson Reflections:

— Are my students' computations accurate and can they clearly explain how and why?
— Do my students see the relationships among different representations of this pattern?
— Are my students ready to create their own growing patterns?

(continued)

Figure 12-2 (*continued*)

Exploring the H Pattern

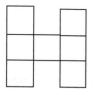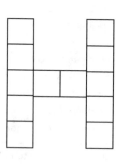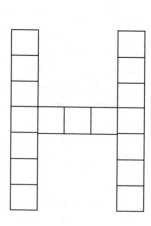

Stage 1   Stage 2   Stage 3

Stages 1, 2, and 3 of the H pattern are shown above.

1. Draw a picture of stages 4 and 5 of the H pattern.

2. Create a table showing the relationship between the stage number and the total number of tiles for the first seven stages of the H pattern.

3. Look for a pattern and predict the number of tiles needed to create stage 10 of the pattern.

4. Write a rule that tells the number of tiles needed for any stage of the H pattern. Justify your reasoning.

5. Can any stage of this pattern contain exactly 152 tiles? Explain why or why not.

Accessible Mathematics

We All *Have a Role to Play and* Teachers Can't Do It Alone

13

On one level the strategies discussed in this book can seem very clear and very straightforward. But taken together, they represent a significant change in practice for many teachers. It is unreasonable to expect to see these strategies broadly implemented just because they are posted or advocated—or even if this book is widely distributed. More realistically, the instructional shifts being advocated require understanding, attention, and commitment on the part of many beyond the classroom.

Consider what we would expect to see *students* doing in an effective classroom:

- engaging in tasks that promote mathematical reasoning, communication, and problem solving
- interacting with each other, as well as working independently
- using textbooks as one of many instructional resources
- using manipulative materials, technology, and other tools when appropriate
- applying mathematical ideas to real-life situations and embedding mathematics in realistic contexts

- communicating verbally and in writing to explain their reasoning and their solutions
- proposing alternative approaches and challenging, defending, confirming, and verifying possible solutions.

It should be clear that these behaviors depend directly on what teachers do and on the classroom routines and practices they establish. In an effective classroom where students regularly exhibit the above behaviors, one would expect their *teachers* to be

- setting high expectations for students in word, tone, and deed
- aligning daily instruction with the district and state curriculum framework and the skills and concepts assessed on the high-stakes accountability tests
- providing students with rich mathematical tasks and problems that constitute the heart of all lessons
- promoting collaboration and communication in pairs, small groups, and whole-class settings
- encouraging students to find alternative approaches and solutions
- seeking answers to "Why?" and expecting that students explain their reasoning
- using the textbook as one of several resources for planning and conducting instruction
- modeling and encouraging the use of manipulative materials, calculators, and other tools as appropriate to enhance the development of mathematical understanding
- embedding assessment opportunities into all activities to monitor instruction
- moving around the room, monitoring instruction, keeping students on task, and assessing individual progress
- working collaboratively with school and grade-level colleagues to solve common problems, plan collaboratively, and provide mutual support.

Just as students operate within the context of a classroom, teachers operate within the context of a school. Accordingly, to ensure that teachers are able to act in these ways, *principals* should be

Accessible Mathematics

- knowledgeable about district mathematics standards, the expectations of the high-stakes accountability tests, and standards-based instructional materials that support the curriculum
- setting clear expectations for curriculum and instruction and communicating these expectations frequently to students, teachers, and parents
- monitoring daily instruction to ensure that students are actively engaged in worthwhile mathematical tasks and that assessing understanding is embedded in all activities
- assisting teachers and other professional staff in providing rich mathematical tasks and problems that constitute the heart of all lessons
- ensuring professional interaction among teachers by facilitating ongoing sharing of ideas, strategies, experiences, and materials through classroom visitations, peer observations, and faculty discussions
- providing the resources needed to ensure that teachers have the instructional materials necessary to implement the mathematics program
- using faculty meetings to address instructional issues and improvement
- using student achievement data to build action plans for improvement
- supporting and encouraging teachers to take risks and try new approaches.

And just as teachers operate within the context of a school, principals operate within the context of a district. Principals are no more or less likely than teachers to implement these practices unless district-level *administrators and supervisors* are

- knowledgeable about district mathematics standards, the expectations of the high-stakes accountability tests, and standards-based instructional materials that support the curriculum
- establishing a comprehensive K–12 mathematics curriculum that is aligned with the state framework and tests

- ensuring that principals have the necessary professional development to carry out their instructional leadership responsibilities effectively
- providing time for principals to work collaboratively on instructional issues
- providing resources and encouragement for high-quality professional development at the school level
- ensuring that principals have the resources needed to provide sufficient instructional materials to implement the mathematics program
- working with principals to analyze and use achievement data to build action plans for improvement
- supporting and encouraging principals to take risks and try new approaches.

In other words, we are an interdependent system. We are all in this improvement business together. Students won't behave in mathematically and educationally productive ways unless their teachers regularly encourage and support their efforts to do so. In similar fashion, most teachers are unlikely to adopt the practices discussed here unless they are regularly encouraged and supported by their principals. And it follows that few principals are likely to put mathematics instruction on the front burner unless and until this emphasis is regularly encouraged and supported by district-level administrators.

Too often we blame the kids or bemoan the teachers or castigate the administrators. Instead, the only effective mindset is the attitude, from top to bottom, of "We're in this together" and consensus that improving student achievement requires specific actions on the part of all.

And if we are, indeed, all in this together, then professional collaboration is a necessity. Sure we can expect to find a scattering of implementation in some classrooms and by some teachers, but any school- or department-wide implementation of the shifts discussed in this book requires collaboration and professional interaction. In schools that are working and best serving students mathematically, one can expect that many of the following activities are in place and regularly implemented.

In the Area of Curriculum

1. There are annual collegial discussions of the following for each grade and each course.
   - What works, what doesn't work?
   - What math, what order, what's skipped, what's supplemented?
   - What's expected, what's not expected?
   - What's on the common final/grade-level CRT?
   - What gets recorded in a written action plan?

2. There are periodic mathematics strand or topic discussions (algebra, fractions, statistics):
   - What works, what doesn't work?
   - Appropriate/inappropriate course/grade placement and overlaps

3. There are "baby vs. bath water" discussions and decisions about specific topics.
   - What's still important, what's no longer important?
   - Do I care whether my own kids can do this?

4. There are common readings and focused discussions to truly build communities of learners.
   - To what degree are we already addressing the issue or issues raised in this article?
   - In what ways are we not addressing all or part of this issue?
   - What are the reasons why we are not addressing this issue?
   - What steps can we take to make improvements and narrow the gap between what we are currently doing and what we should be doing?

5. Teachers collectively and collaboratively give themselves permission to adjust the curriculum on the assumption that they own the curriculum to a greater degree than most assume.

In the Area of Teaching and Learning

1. Frequent classroom visits are used to broaden perspectives and stimulate discussions.
   - Typical and demonstration classes
   - Building a sense that we're all in this together and face common problems

2. Teachers create videotapes of their lessons for collegial review and discussion.

3. Teachers collaboratively craft powerful lessons that are drawn in part from such sites as www.nctm.org/illuminations and www.mathforum.com or that support "Here's the data, what's the math and what are the questions that best elicit the math?" instruction.

4. Teachers regularly review and analyze student work.
   - Look at what my kids did!
   - What does work like this tell us we ought to do?

5. There is an annual review of common finals/grade-level criterion-reference test data.

6. There are intense discussions about what's on the test to examine the truism that "What we assess and how we assess communicate what we value."
   - Types of items/tasks/questions
   - Content and processes measured
   - Contexts, complexity, appropriateness, memorization required

7. Time is set aside for annual action-planning sessions.
   - What are we doing well?
   - What can we do to expand what is working?
   - What are we not doing as well?
   - What can we do to improve what is not working as well?

In the Area of Professional Growth

1. Faculty, grade-level, and department meetings are used as opportunities to inform, stimulate, challenge, and grow by adapting the "faculty seminar" model and using, for example, chapters from this book or the material in the Appendixes as starting points for discussion and reflection.

2. There are well-developed and intensive induction procedures, processes, and traditions for all first- and second-year teachers.

3. There are annual "What do the data tell us?" sessions to review what is working and what is not.

4. There are frequent "What do the videotapes tell us?" sessions that might compare and contrast two higher-level classes/courses with two lower-level classes/courses.

5. There are discussions about the policies in place and their implications, including such topics as
   - Algebra I placement
   - grouping by reading levels
   - heterogeneous grouping mandates
   - pull-out programs

   In other words, as professionals, we adapt the following mindsets.

- We're all in this together and need to work collaboratively to serve all students.
- People can't do what they can't envision, and people won't do what they don't understand; therefore, colleagues help each other envision and understand.
- No one knows it all or has all the answers; therefore, there is a need for differentiation and teamwork.
- Professional sharing is part of my job.
- Professional growth, and admitting we need to grow, is a core aspect of being a professional.

Conclusion

Instructional Productivity

In a factory or on a farm, productivity is measured in terms of the quantity of goods produced per unit of worker-hour input. In a business, productivity is measured in terms of the quantity of work completed or dollars earned per hour or per employee. In our schools, where it has rarely been a serious consideration, productivity is the amount of student academic achievement or the degree of academic improvement per year per teacher or per school. In the simplest of all terms, schools today are being asked to be more productive. And more and more, they are asked to be much more mathematically productive!

We are being asked to ensure that more students master more mathematics. Accomplishing this—that is, being more productive—will not result from exhortation or fiat. It won't occur when we try to ram the same math down the same throats with the same instructional practices. Instead, as we have seen, increasing the productivity of our mathematics programs and instruction requires deliberate shifts in what mathematics we expect our students to master, shifts in when we expect them to master it, and most important, shifts in how we teach it.

It is frequently noted that "if we continue to do what we've always done, we'll continue to get what we've already gotten." This aphorism certainly applies to teaching students mathematics. There is no way, as a school, a district, a state, or a nation, that we will ever reach our professed goal of mathematical proficiency for all by continuing to do the same things in the same ways we've always done them. Doing nothing or continuing to do the same things in the face of mediocre achievement outcomes is simply irresponsible and unprofessional, and it will not help more students learn mathematics.

Alternatively, the more powerful aphorism is acting on the fact that "if . . . what we've always done is no longer working, then we have no choice but to change some of what we do and some of how we go about doing it." This book has argued that we will be much more productive when we change some of what we do and some of how we do it. Among these powerful shifts are to

- incorporate ongoing cumulative review into daily instruction
- parallel the literal, inferential, and evaluative comprehension of reading instruction in mathematics
- regularly draw pictures, create mental images, and rely on multiple representations of mathematical ideas
- use explanations, classroom discussion, and writing assignments to create language-rich mathematics classrooms
- use every appropriate opportunity to develop number sense in our students
- build from the data contained in graphs, charts, and tables to engage students and ground the mathematics
- tie the math to questions such as "How big?" "How much?" and "How far?" that elevate the measurement strand
- minimize what it is no longer important for students to know
- embed the math in contexts/problems
- make "Why?" "How do you know?" and "Can you explain?" classroom mantras
- plan our lessons and units far more deliberately
- significantly enhance the quality and quantity of our professional collaboration.

As noted in the introduction, we really do have many of the answers we need to make significant gains in our productivity. The task we face is to broadly institutionalize these answers in the thousands of school districts, the tens of thousands of schools, and the hundreds of thousands of classrooms where mathematics is taught and must be taught better.

Appendix 1

A Crib Sheet for Raising Mathematics Achievement for All

What mathematics do we focus on?

- Core mathematical concepts
- Key skills with understanding
- Facility with terms, vocabulary, and notation
- Ability to apply the mathematics and solve problems

How do we teach it?

- Ask "Why?"
- Alternative approaches
- Multiple representations
- Language-rich classrooms
- Contexts
- Connections
- Ongoing cumulative review

Why should we bother?

- Supports sense-making for all
- Supports understanding by more students
- Mathematically empowers students

Appendix 2

A Model Vision of Effective Teaching and Learning of Mathematics[1]

An effective and coherent mathematics program should be *guided* by a clear set of content standards, but it must be *grounded* in a clear and shared vision of teaching and learning—the two critical reciprocal actions that link teachers and students and largely determine educational impact. Curriculum, materials, professional development, assessment, and cultivating broad programmatic support are all necessary components of the educational enterprise, but they have little real impact unless they are effectively enacted in each and every classroom where learning is facilitated, supported, and maximized.

Accordingly, to ground and guide the development and implementation of a highly effective school mathematics program for *all* students, we describe a research-based vision of teaching and learning with twelve interrelated characteristics of effective instruction in mathematics. We hope that this vision will define and inspire excellence in classrooms where mathematics is taught and learned.

---

[1] Adapted from work the author did in conjunction with the Jefferson County Public Schools and the Jefferson County Teachers Association with the support of the General Electric Foundation's Developing Futures initiative.

Effective mathematics instruction is thoughtfully planned.

An effective lesson provides multiple opportunities for student learning and must be carefully planned. The days of minimalist lesson plans like "Examples 1 and 2 on page 154" or "Lesson 6-4: vocabulary, discussion, practice, homework" do not adequately reflect the demands and expectations teachers face. Rather, prior to teaching a lesson, teachers should be empowered and expected to

- have a clear understanding of the specific learning expectations for their students and how and where these expectations fit into the larger instructional unit
- select and try out the set of problems, tasks, and/or activities that support the specific learning expectations
- identify a set of key questions and consider the required explanations that support the problems, tasks, and/or activities to be used
- consider the errors that students are likely to make and the misconceptions they are likely to have, and prepare strategies that address these errors and misconceptions
- identify the means by which the degree of student learning will be determined.

The heart of effective mathematics instruction is an emphasis on problem solving, reasoning, and sense-making.

Nearly every survey of business and industry addresses the critical need for current and prospective workers to be able to reason, question, and solve problems. Thus the focus on problem solving as the heart of mathematics and the focus on inquiry as the heart of science are societal, as well as educational, imperatives. However, beyond just rhetoric, effective instruction must consistently include opportunities for students to formulate questions and problems, make hypotheses and conjectures, gather and analyze data, and draw and justify conclusions. This is why students in effective classrooms regularly encounter questions like "Why?" "How do you know?" and "Can you explain that?"

Effective mathematics instruction balances and blends conceptual understanding and procedural skills.

Real mathematical literacy is as much about understanding the concept of division, knowing when and why to divide, and being able to interpret the meaning of a remainder as it is about merely knowing how to use an algorithm to find a quotient. Too often, the focus of instruction is on the one right way to get a single right answer, at the expense of understanding why this is the appropriate mathematics, how it is related to other mathematics, and when such mathematics should be used. For this reason, effective instruction balances a focus on conceptual understanding (such as the meaning of area and perimeter and how they are related) with a focus on procedural skill (such as how to find the area and perimeter of plane figures).

Effective mathematics instruction relies on alternative approaches and multiple representations.

At nearly every moment in nearly every class, we know that many students are not processing the content in the way the teacher is processing the content. For example, the teacher may be visualizing "three-quarters" as three out of four slices of a small pizza, while one student "sees" three quarters or 75 cents, another student "sees" three red balloons out of a total of four, and still another student "sees" three-quarters of an inch on a ruler. Effective instruction recognizes that students conceptualize mathematical and scientific concepts in different, but often equally appropriate, ways. Effective instruction incorporates deliberate attention to such multiple representations, including concrete materials, and to alternative approaches to accommodate the diverse learning styles within every class.

Effective mathematics instruction uses contexts and connections to engage students and increase the relevance of what is being learned.

Teachers have a choice. They can rely on abstractions and rules that are rarely connected to realistic situations or common contexts and ask students the equivalent of finding F when $S = 81$ in the function $F = 4 (S - 65) + 10$. Or teachers can take these abstractions and embed them in realistic contexts and problem situations that bring the mathematics and science to life. In this example, that might mean telling students that the speeding fine in a particular state is "$4 for every mile per hour over the 65 mph speed limit plus a $10 handling fee for the Police Department" and asking them to determine first the fine when a driver is going 81 mph and then the speed of a driver who received a fine of $102. Next consider using a graphing calculator or computer software to represent this function in a table and a graph as well as symbolically, showing where and how the "point" (81, 74) exists within each representation.

Effective mathematics instruction provides frequent opportunities for students to communicate their reasoning and engage in productive discourse.

The active, engaged, thinking classroom is a classroom of questions and answers, of inquiries and explanations, of conjectures and justifications, and of written and oral discourse. We know that writing helps to clarify our thinking and that teaching another strengthens our own learning. That is why effective classrooms are often vibrant environments of student communication in the form of explanations, dialogues, arguments, and presentations.

Effective mathematics instruction incorporates ongoing cumulative review.

Almost no one masters something new after one or two lessons and one or two homework assignments. That is why one of the most effective strategies for fostering mastery and retention of critical skills is daily, cumulative review at the beginning of every lesson. Teachers do this as part of a daily warm-up or as "bell-work" that focuses on recent instruction or as a daily "mini-quiz" containing 4 to 6 problems that keep skills sharp, review vocabulary, and reinforce conceptual understanding.

Effective mathematics instruction employs technology to enhance learning.

Calculators, computers, and scientific instruments are increasingly important tools for supporting learning and making instruction more relevant. Graphing calculators that link symbolic, tabular, and graphical representations of functions help students develop critical understandings of algebra. Geometry software and scientific simulation software enable students to create mathematical and scientific environments and to analyze the impact of changes in selected conditions. Electronic blackboards significantly enhance the impact of such software. But it is not the mere use of technology that enhances learning, any more than it is the use of manipulative materials that "teach." Rather, it is the appropriate, planned, and deliberate use of technology to support the development of mathematical understanding that affects learning.

Effective mathematics instruction maximizes time on task.

Videos of classes are striking in their variation in the number of minutes of engaged time on task—that is, in the use of time for activities that engage learners and support learning. Some classes begin even before the bell rings with warm-up work posted or distributed at the door, use efficient and established routines to go over homework, transition smoothly from one segment of the lesson to another, keep the focus on student work and student thinking for extended periods of time, are rarely interrupted, do not confuse class work with homework, and still allocate time to building positive relationships with students. In this way, a 45-minute class can easily provide more than 40 minutes of engaged time on task. Other classes, when observed or captured on videotape, reveal as much as 20 or more minutes frittered away with organizational matters, frequent interruptions, poor transitions, and off-task chatter.

Effective mathematics instruction uses multiple forms of assessment and uses the results of this assessment to adjust instruction.

When our focus shifts from what was taught to what was learned, the focus must also shift to assessing what has been learned. Although tests and quizzes will continue to be important components of assessment, it is how the results of these quizzes and tests are used to assess the impact of teaching, plan re-teaching, prepare individual instruction, and design additional diagnosis that translates assessment into better teaching and learning. In addition, effective teachers use observations, class work, projects, and similar vehicles to monitor the quality of learning. Finally, the results of a carefully aligned system of unit tests and end-of-grade and end-of-course assessments are regularly analyzed to make curricular and instructional modifications.

Effective mathematics instruction integrates the characteristics of this vision to ensure student mastery of grade-level standards.

The often elusive goal of assisting all students to achieve mastery requires a coherent and supportive program that aligns a vision, a set of standards, instructional materials, assessments, collegial sharing, and professional development. Moving from mastery by some to truly ensuring mastery by all requires shifts in mindsets to align with this vision, shifts in curriculum expectations, shifts in instructional practices, and shifts in allocations of resources. It requires a deep commitment to quality and a non-negotiable belief that all students can learn mathematics.

Effective teachers of mathematics reflect on their teaching, individually and collaboratively, and make revisions to enhance student learning.

Finally, effective teachers replay their instruction, reflect on what appeared to work and what was more problematic, and examine student responses and work as part of an ongoing cycle of plan–teach–reflect–refine and plan all over again. Moreover, effective teachers work collaboratively with colleagues on issues of the mathematics embedded in the instructional tasks that are used, the pedagogical features of the instruction we conduct, and the student learning evidenced by analysis of student work.

On the one hand, we know with certainty that the elements of this vision do not get implemented by exhortation. We know that people will not do what they cannot envision and cannot do what they do not understand. And we know that the lack of a clear and shared vision commonly results in incoherent—often conflicting—policies and a widespread perception that "this too will pass."

On the other hand, we also know that once a broadly shared understanding and acceptance of the elements of this vision of effective teaching and learning are in place, school districts, schools, teachers, and parents have a common platform on which to organize, structure, and improve a high-quality mathematics program.

Appendix 3

Research Matters/Teach Mathematics Right the First Time[1]

— STEVE LEINWAND AND STEVE FLEISCHMAN

In mathematics instruction, a chasm exists between research and practice. For evidence of this gap, look no further than the mismatch between what research says about developing students' conceptual mathematics understanding and what we actually do. An example is the way we teach math content in elementary and middle schools. A growing body of promising research shows that if initial instruction focuses exclusively on procedural skills, then students may have difficulty developing an understanding of math concepts.

Listen to 7th graders define perimeter as "adding up all the numbers," and watch as their teacher struggles, often unsuccessfully, to move these students toward more appropriate understandings: that perimeter is actually the distance around an object, relates to the words *border* and *surrounding*, and is a special case of measuring length. Unfortunately, many people will blame this situation on the "mathematical weaknesses" of the students, or even of the teacher, rather than on instructional sequencing that flies in the face of research.

---

[1]From Leinwand, Steve, and Steve Fleischman. *Educational Leadership,* September 2004. *Teaching for Meaning* 62(1): 88–89.

What We Know

Richard Skemp (1987) coined the terms *instrumental practices* and *relational practices* to differentiate two approaches to teaching and learning. Instrumental practices involve memorizing and routinely applying procedures and formulas. These practices focus on what to do and how to get answers. In contrast, relational practices emphasize the *why* of learning. These practices involve explaining, reasoning, and relying on multiple representations—that is, on teaching for meaning and helping students develop their own understanding of content.

Since the 1980s, several studies have examined the role and impact of instrumental and relational practices on student achievement outcomes. Although the research base is somewhat limited and should be replicated to validate the findings, results consistently point to the importance of using relational practices for teaching mathematics. In the existing research, students who learn rules before they learn concepts tend to score significantly lower than do students who learn concepts first.

For example, Kieran (1984) looked at two groups of students learning to solve simple equations, such as $6 + x = 18$. One group was taught procedures (subtract 6 from both sides); the other was not. Both groups then received instruction about the meaning of variables and equations. Next, they used trial and error to balance an equation. On post-tests, the students who received only meaningful, or relational, instruction performed better in applying the procedure and solving the equations. In contrast, the students who first received procedural instruction on how to solve an equation tended to resist new ideas and appeared to apply procedures without understanding.

Wearne and Hiebert (1988) investigated the effectiveness of different approaches for teaching decimal concepts. They suggested that

> students who have already routinized rules without establishing connections between symbols [and what they mean] will be less likely to engage in the [conceptual] processes than students who are encountering decimals for the first time. (p. 374)

Perhaps most convincing is the work of Pesek and Kirshner (2000). They studied students who were learning about area and perimeter and concluded that "initial rote learning of a concept can create interference to later meaningful learning" (p. 537). Students who were exposed to instrumental instruction before they received relational instruction "achieved no more, and most probably less, conceptual understanding than students exposed only to the relational unit." Even more telling was the way students in the two study groups approached solving problems. Students who learned area and perimeter as a set of how-to rules referred to formulas, operations, and fixed procedures to solve problems. In contrast, students whose initial experiences were relational used conceptual and flexible methods to develop solutions.

This research strongly reinforces our understanding that the form of instruction humorously but accurately characterized as *yours is not to reason why, just invert and multiply* may not enhance the performance of many students. Alternatively, instruction that places a premium from the start on meaning and conceptual understanding may improve classroom productivity.

What You Can Do

Mathematics teachers can take simple and immediate steps to put the gist of this research into practice.

- Promote students' discussion of making meaning by posing open-ended questions: *Why do you think that? Can you explain your reasoning? How do you know that?*
- Make explicit connections and incorporate pictures, concrete materials, and role playing as part of instruction so that students have multiple representations of concepts and alternative paths to developing understanding.
- Avoid instruction focused on teaching a single correct approach to arrive at a single correct answer.

Educators Take Note

In his review of the scientific research on mathematics instruction, Grover Whitehurst, the director of the U.S. Department of Education's Institute of Educational Sciences, rightly points out that educators should be wary about basing instructional practices on potentially unsubstantiated translations of study findings (2003). Whitehurst adds, however, that "literature demonstrates the limits of generalization of math skills that can occur when instruction focuses exclusively on learning facts and procedures."

This month's column offers some research-based guidelines for mathematics instruction in the hope that they will support improved student achievement. The research message is strong: Teach for meaning initially, or risk never getting students beyond a superficial understanding that leaves them unprepared to apply their learning.

References

Kieran, C. (1984). A comparison between novice and more-expert algebra students on tasks dealing with the equivalence of equations. In J. M. Moser (Ed.), *Proceedings of the sixth annual meeting of the North American chapter of the International Group for the Psychology of Mathematics Education* (pp. 83–91). Madison, WI: University of Wisconsin.

Pesek, D., & Kirshner, D. (2000). Interference of instrumental instruction in subsequent relational learning. *Journal for Research in Mathematics Education, 31*, 524–540.

Skemp, R. (1987). *The psychology of learning mathematics*. Hillsdale, NJ: Erlbaum.

Wearne, D., & Hiebert, J. (1988). A cognitive approach to mathematics instruction: Testing a local theory using decimal numbers. *Journal for Research in Mathematics Education, 19*, 371–384.

Whitehurst, G. (2003, February). *Research on mathematics instruction* [Online]. Paper presented at the Secretary's Summit on Mathematics, Washington, DC. Available: www.ed.gov/rschstat/research/progs/mathscience/whitehurst.html

Appendix 4

Classroom Realities
We Do Not Often Talk About[1]

A fter spending time in diverse schools, I often return to the *Profes-sional Standards for Teaching Mathematics* (NCTM 1991) to help sort through what I have seen and heard. I use the Standards document to track the gap between our vision and the day-to-day realities I observe. A well-worn touchstone is Standard 6: Analysis of Teaching and Learning, which states the following:

> The teacher of mathematics should engage in ongoing analysis of teaching and learning by
>
> - observing, listening to, and gathering other information about students to assess what they are learning
> - examining effects of the tasks, discourse, and learning environment on students' mathematical knowledge, skills, and dispositions.

That is our vision. However, listen in on conversations in the teachers' lounge, and you mostly hear about how exhausted we are by trying to make things work. Occasionally, you will hear about a nugget of

---

[1]Leinwand, S. (1998, February). "Classroom Realities We Do Not Often Talk About." *Mathematics Teaching in the Middle School*. Reston, VA: National Council of Teachers of Mathematics.

success, a tidbit of what worked, or a smiling snippet of pride in another small classroom victory.

Rarely, however, do you hear much analysis of, or reflection on, many of our day-to-day realities. Some topics never seem to arise in the discussions. After years of participating in, and listening to, teachers' room discussions, I am struck by how rarely we talk about our mistakes or about what did not work last period or about how successful or unsuccessful we are in converting the blank stares of confusion into knowing nods of understanding.

Of course, it is hard to admit mistakes and errors. It is even harder to delve publicly into pedagogical issues that relate to our individual effectiveness. But look at how much students learn when we analyze and discuss mistakes, misunderstandings, and errors. Consider how much students learn when faulty reasoning is defined and corrected or inappropriate strategies are replaced with more appropriate ones. Should not the same analysis and discussion apply to our work?

My own pet issues revolve around the inconsistency of the impact of what we do, the crucial need to incorporate alternative approaches into everything we do, and the mistakes we make in the classroom. These areas are three pieces of every teacher's reality about which I wish we were more open. I believe that they need to be discussed more often, more openly, and more collegially. So let me try to stimulate such discussions.

1. *Just because it worked once . . . .* One of the first important lessons we learn about classroom realities is that just because something worked first period is no guarantee that it will work fifth period. And just because something worked last year is no guarantee that it will work this year. Conversely, just because something blew up in our faces last year or last period is no reason not to try it again this year or next period—perhaps in the same way or perhaps in some modified fashion. The fact is that classroom dynamics and the unique personalities of each class are often far more powerful determinants of the success or failure of a lesson or an activity than our own plans and actions.

   Yet how often do our professional conversations focus on these shared experiences? How often do we mutter in frustration when one of our favorite activities fails to "turn on" a particular class? And how often do we omit a particular activity after one failure instead of reflecting on what went wrong and trying it again?

Wouldn't teaching be far less frustrating if we knew that our colleagues were dealing with exactly the same experiences?

2. ***Who really understands?*** One of the starkest realities all teachers face is the fact that at any given moment, in any given class, more than half of our students are very like not seeing, feeling, or processing the mathematics that we are teaching in the same way that we are seeing, feeling, and processing it. Call it "learning styles" or "alternative modes of learning"; it comes down to different brains working in different ways. When we have one-fourth of a pizza pie shaded on the chalkboard, one of our students sees only the numbers 1 over 4. Another sees a quarter with George Washington on one side and an eagle on the other. Still another is far more comfortable with a small mark on his or her ruler between 0 and 1. Similarly, whereas we may be perfectly comfortable with the symbolic abstraction of a linear function, some of our students need the spreadsheet or tabular representation of the same equation, and others see the line that represents the function on a set of coordinate axes. Just think how often we hear, "They just don't get it!"

That is why effective teachers never rely on the one right way to do a problem. That is why effective teachers encourage alternative approaches and employ multiple representations of key concepts to broaden the likelihood of understanding—even approaches and representations with which they themselves are not comfortable.

Again, what better way to strengthen instruction than by engaging in collegial discussion about how best to foster understanding? How better to broaden our own personal repertoire of approaches than from our colleagues and from an examination of student work?

3. ***Mistakes.*** Another aspect of teaching that we all recognize, but seldom talk about, is how rare the perfect class is. In fact, we know that it is almost impossible to teach a 45-minute class without making at least two mistakes. Usually, one mistake is mathematical and careless because we are thinking two steps ahead. Sometimes our students catch our mistakes, and sometimes the errors sit on the chalkboard unnoticed until no one agrees with the final answer. The second mistake is usually pedagogical and results

from calling on the wrong student at the wrong time or assigning the wrong problem at the wrong time, engendering far more confusion than we would prefer. To make this situation worse, we have learned that when a principal or supervisor is in the room, the likelihood that we will make an additional mistake significantly increases. And if we are using technology, it is essentially impossible to avoid hitting the wrong key at least once!

Why, if such mistakes are almost inevitable, do we get so embarrassed by them? Why do we expect perfection from ourselves when we know that errors can be such powerful learning opportunities? Why are we so hard on ourselves over one error in judgment, when fifty other quick decisions worked fine? And why are we so reluctant to share these experiences with colleagues who are having exactly the same experiences with their classes?

The popularity of NCTM's *Curriculum and Evaluation Standards for School Mathematics* (1989) vis-à-vis the *Professional Standards for Teaching Mathematics* (1991) reminds us how much more comfortable we are talking about curriculum than about pedagogy. I think that teachers' lounges and faculty dining rooms and departmental offices are great places to engage one another in the less comfortable, but far more nitty-gritty, discussions of what works, what does not work, and why. I also think that such discussions are invaluable vehicles for reducing our isolation and for acknowledging how complex our jobs are and how exhausting it is to do them well.

References

National Council of Teachers of Mathematics (NCTM). *Curriculum and Evaluation Standards for School Mathematics.* Reston, VA: NCTM, 1989.

National Council of Teachers of Mathematics (NCTM). *Professional Standards for Teaching Mathematics.* Reston, VA: NCTM, 1991.

Appendix 5

Learning from Singapore Math[1]

— STEVEN LEINWAND AND ALAN L. GINSBURG
The United States could benefit from looking at five elements driving the program's success.

As the United States strives to improve student performance in mathematics, it is not surprising that the small country of Singapore—with its highly regarded mathematics program familiarly known as Singapore Math—has attracted so much attention. After all, Singapore students have the enviable record of scoring first in the world in mathematics proficiency on the past three Trends in International Mathematics and Science Studies (TIMSS), soundly beating their U.S. counterparts.

But this world-class performance did not happen by accident. It is proof that taking a few crucial actions can pay rich dividends in terms of significantly raising student achievement. In fact, Singapore's mathematics and science achievement in the early 1990s was comparable to the consistently mediocre achievement of the United States (International Association for the Evaluation of Educational Achievement, 1988). However, the country's poor performance served as the impetus for concerted national efforts that have resulted in its current success in mathematics.

---

[1] From Leinwand, Steven, and Alan L. Ginsburg. *Educational Leadership,* November 2007. 65(3): 32–36.

Of course, all international comparisons need to be made with great care, given the vast cultural, governmental, and demographic differences among countries. In the case of Singapore and the United States, however, these differences are often overstated. Some claim that Singapore's student population is not as diverse as that of the United States. In fact, almost a quarter of Singapore's students are Malay or Indian, with the majority of its population being Chinese. Others argue that with a population of only 4.1 million people, Singapore cannot be reasonably compared with the United States, with its population of 300 million. Nevertheless, Singapore's population makes the country only a little smaller than Chicago and more populous than approximately one-half of U.S. states.

Winning the international horse race in mathematics should not receive as much attention as the specific elements of the program and the policies that support its implementation. These can be powerful models for a reasoned analysis of how to make U.S. mathematics programs far more productive. The following five elements have contributed to the success of Singapore Math.

Element 1: An Organizing Framework

In the United States, a shared common vision for school mathematics does not exist. By default, the National Council of Teachers of Mathematics has come closest to articulating a national vision, built most recently in *Principles and Standards for School Mathematics* (2000) on two lists of standards—one for content and one for processes. In contrast, Singapore's guiding framework presents a balanced, integrated vision that connects and describes skills, concepts, processes, attitudes, and metacognition (see Figure A-1). Instead of implicitly giving equal weight to content and process components and failing to make explicit the crucial connections between them—the current situation in the United States—Singapore places problem solving at the center of the framework and uses a pentagon to represent the connections and integration of program goals.

It is interesting to note the similarity between the Singapore framework and the five strands of mathematical proficiency—

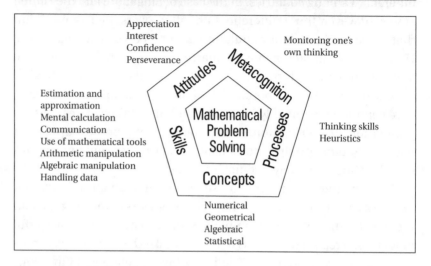

Source: From *Mathematics Syllabus Primary*, p. 6, 2001, Singapore: Curriculum Planning and Development Division, Ministry of Education, Singapore. Copyright 2001 by the Curriculum Planning and Development Division. Adapted with permission.

conceptual understanding, procedural fluency, strategic competence, adaptive reasoning, and productive disposition—that are presented in the National Research Council's *Adding It Up: Helping Children Learn Mathematics* (2001), a source too infrequently consulted by designers of mathematics programs.

The lesson to be learned is that the very narrowness and disconnected nature of the organizing structure of mathematics education in the United States prevents us from developing a stronger and more effective instructional program.

Element 2: Alignment

One of the most significant differences between the two countries has to do with alignment: The elements of Singapore Math *deliberately* align with one another. It is no secret that in the United States, teachers face a fragmented array of "masters," including the textbook, the local curriculum, the state curriculum, and, most powerfully, state tests. Not only are these elements poorly aligned, but also their competing and often conflicting demands make programmatic focus and coherence nearly impossible to attain.

The wide range of expectations among the 50 states concerning mastery of key mathematics skill standards illustrates this lack of alignment. For example, according to the Center for the Study of Mathematics Curriculum, one state expects fluency in addition and subtraction of fractions in 4th grade; 15 states expect this of their students in 5th grade; 20 states, in 6th grade; and 6 states, in 7th grade (Reys et al., 2006).

In Singapore, each element of the system—the framework, a common set of national standards, texts, tests, and teacher preparation programs—is carefully aligned to clear and common goals. The United States is unlikely to achieve world-class status in mathematics as long as the patchwork of 50 different state frameworks and assessment instruments remains misaligned with the major textbooks, which are designed to be all things to all people.

Element 3: Focus

The degree to which the often-used phrase "a mile wide and an inch deep" applies to the typical U.S. mathematics curriculum becomes clear when analyzing Singapore Math. Typical U.S. state mathematics frameworks delineate many more topics and outcomes per grade level than Singapore does. For example, regarding mathematics standards in grades 1–6, Singapore covers an average of 15 topics per grade level (Ministry of Education, Singapore, 2001), compared with Florida's 54 and New Jersey's 50. Singapore's success suggests that reducing the repetition of topics from year to year, particularly within the number and geometry strands, would enable the curriculum to progress at a faster pace and with better results. It is interesting to note that the two states that delineate the least number of topics per grade level—North Carolina, with 18, and Texas, with 19—are recognized for their successful performance in the National Assessment of Educational Progress.

An analysis of 3rd grade textbooks (Ginsburg, Leinwand, Anstrom, & Pollock, 2005) shows that the most commonly used elementary textbooks in the United States compound the problem of a lack of coherence and focus. For example, the textbook commonly used in Singapore at that grade level has 496 pages, 14 chapters, 42 lessons, and an average of 12 pages per lesson. Compare that with the 3rd grade Scott Foresman textbook, with its 729 pages, 32 chapters, 164 lessons, and 4 pages per lesson. Singapore's success is likely attributable, in part, to the substantial number of pages it allots per lesson (12 as opposed to 4 in the Scott Foresman textbook) and to the fact that it focuses on far fewer lessons per grade level than U.S. textbooks do (42 lessons as opposed to 164). This has resulted in much greater mathematical focus at each grade level.

Element 4: Multiple Models

Many U.S. textbooks are notable for their four-color photographs that relate only tangentially, if at all, to the mathematics at hand. In contrast, Singapore textbooks are notable for their multiple representations and for simple cartoons (see Figure A-2), in which an illustrated figure suggests a strategy ("Divide 18 by 2"); notes an equation; provides information about the problem; or poses questions.

The development of fraction understandings, for example, consistently blends concrete representations (four of six balls are striped), pictorial representations (six of nine congruent regions in a rectangle are shaded), and abstract representations ($\frac{2}{3} = \frac{4}{6} = \frac{6}{9}$). Work with multiplying and dividing by 6 is presented with "$\times 6$" and "$\div 6$" input-output "machines." An input of 5 in the $\times 6$ machine results in an output of 30; an input of 30 in the $\div 6$ machine results in an output of 5. This representation is followed by a 5-unit-by-6-unit rectangular array accompanied by a think bubble noting that $5 \times 6 = 6 \times 5$ and by a column of 5 blocks "$\times 6$" resulting in 6 columns of 5 blocks that provide still another pictorial representation of 5×6. Thus, the textbook provides students and teachers with multiple representations on which to build skills and conceptual understanding. In this manner, Singapore textbooks systematically

Appendix 5

1. Robert has $18.

He has twice as much money as Sarah has.
How much money does Sarah have?

$18

Robert

Sarah

?

18 ÷ 2 = _____

Sarah has $ _____

Divide
18 by 2

support instruction consistent with research on how the progression from concrete to pictorial to abstract enhances learning (Ginsburg et al., 2005).

In addition, most U.S. mathematics programs superficially jump around from counters to number lines to base-10 blocks to teach number concepts and from area models to strip models to number line models to teach fractions. In contrast, Singapore's program consistently uses the bar or strip model as a pictorial model for parts and wholes in addition, subtraction, multiplication, division, fractions, ratios, and percentages (see Figure A-2). This consistent use of a single powerful model provides a unifying pedagogical structure entirely missing in U.S. mathematics programs.

Element 5: Rich Problems

We know that in reading instruction, higher-order questions and more advanced text help develop stronger comprehension. Analogously, more complex multi-step problems support stronger mathematical development. However, the vast majority of problems in U.S. textbooks are one-step exercises that rarely demand anything more than recall and routine application.

Consider this problem from Singapore Math, grade 4:

> Meredith bought $\frac{2}{5}$ kg of shrimps. Courtney bought $\frac{1}{10}$ kg of shrimps less than Meredith.
>
> Find the weight of the shrimps bought by Courtney.
>
> Find the total weight of shrimps bought by both girls.

or this problem from Singapore Math, grade 6:

> The ratio of the number of blue beads to the number of red beads in a jar was 2:5 at first. Ian removed $\frac{1}{4}$ of the blue beads and $\frac{2}{5}$ of the red beads from the jar.
>
> Find the new ratio of the number of blue beads to the number of red beads.
>
> If there were 12 more red beads than blue beads left in the jar, how many beads were removed altogether?

In both cases, as is typical in the Singapore texts, students are expected to complete multi-step problems, apply a range of skills and concepts, and often find intermediate values to arrive at a solution. A steady diet of problems such as these enhances the development of broader and deeper mathematical understanding.

We can see the difference between the Singapore and U.S. approaches in two grade 6 problems about pie charts, one typical of Singapore Math and one typical of a Scott Foresman math textbook (see Figure A-3). The Singapore problem requires about six steps and an understanding that a right angle is 90 degrees and that the two right-angle sectors must be equal and must represent half the total amount of money. The problem also illustrates how Singapore uses problems to reinforce a range of skills and understandings while teaching students how to interpret pie charts.

A pie chart problem typical of Singapore Math:

The pie chart represents the amount of money that a family spends each month.

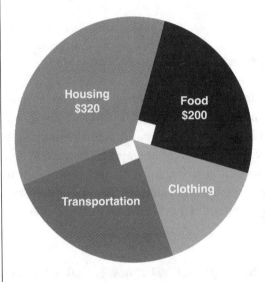

Monthly Family Budget

a. What fraction of the total budget went to transportation?

b. What was the total amount of money the family budgeted for the month?

c. How much money was budgeted for clothing?

d. What was the ratio of the amount budgeted for housing to the amount budgeted for food?

A pie chart problem typical of Scott Foresman–Addison Wesley Math

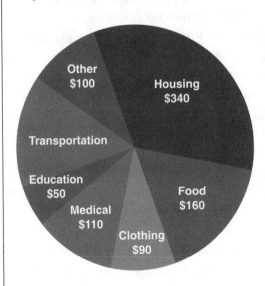

Annual Family Expenses
(for each $1,000)

a. How much does the family spend on transportation for each $1,000?

b. For each $1,000, how much more does the family spend on housing than on food and medical expenses?

c. TEST PREP. If the family spends $4000, about how much is spent on clothing?
1) $100 2) $200 3) $400 4) $1,000

d. For what category does the family spend about three times what it spends on medical expenses?

Compare the richness of this problem with the routine, low-level expectations required by the Scott Foresman problem. It is easy to get a sense of why U.S. students are often deprived of important opportunities to learn.

A Lesson for Us All

Too often in our search for quick fixes, we jump on the latest bandwagon or reach out for the latest fad. It would be unfortunate to react to the United States' problems in mathematics achievement by assuming that the widespread adoption of Singapore Math is the cure-all. Instead, the real value is in the Singapore Math *program*—in the fact that it helps us identify the essential features that the United States needs to adapt and adopt to remain mathematically competitive.

References

Ginsburg, A., Leinwand, S., Anstrom, T., & Pollock, E. (2005). *What the United States can learn from Singapore's world-class mathematics system (and what Singapore can learn from the United States).* Washington, DC: American Institutes for Research.

International Association for the Evaluation of Educational Achievement. (1988). *Science achievement in seventeen countries: A preliminary report.* New York: Pergamon Press.

Ministry of Education, Singapore. (2001). *Primary Mathematics Syllabus.* Singapore: Ministry of Education, Curriculum Planning and Development Division. Available: www1.moe.edu.sg/cpdd/doc/Maths_Pri.pdf

National Council of Teachers of Mathematics. (2000). *Principals and standards for school mathematics.* Reston, VA: Author. Available: www.nctm.org/standards

National Research Council. (2001). *Adding it up: Helping children learn mathematics.* Washington, DC: National Academies Press.

Reys, B., et al. (2006). *The intended mathematics curriculum as represented in state-level curriculum standards: Consensus or confusion?* Center for the Study of Mathematics Curriculum.

25 min

Shannon – PD out of this book

2 copies on Table

Sales force – See Dingles

Why to reference others to do use this book –

Connect HLTA – Help in your work!
Who is audience

NCTM / NCSM

Slides for b.m – make our folks aware

build membership

To share @ NCTM resources

work with Matt –

NCSM "

Electronic folders:

Chrissy Foust Tas

1) NCTM resources

2) membership – he's how you join

3) What's coming up

— URL addresses – digital links

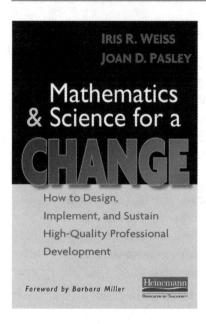

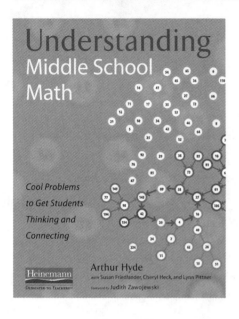